THE SALES PLAN

**The definitive five-step guide to selling.
Learn to generate leads, win new customers and
grow accounts in a changing and competitive world.**

CARLOS HORNER

First published in Great Britain in 2019

ISBN 9781092831864

Refine Business Development Ltd
10 Claro Court
Claro Road
Harrogate, HG1 4BA
www.thesalesplan.co.uk

Table of Contents

Foreword

Why are some businesses good at selling and others poor? It's a question that every entrepreneur has asked themselves at some point in their careers. I was introduced to selling through the world of stock broking, where one of my first jobs was selling equities to institutions. It was at that time I developed the sales skills which have been fundamental in helping me build a range of successful businesses in a variety of sectors.

I am delighted to write this foreword, not just because Carlos has been a friend and colleague for many years, but the subject matter is something close to my heart. I believe that salesmanship is a key skill that should be taught to anyone in business. As without the ability to sell, good businesses struggle and sometimes fail, which should never happen.

Like many entrepreneurs, I succeeded in selling largely due to sheer force of character and dogged perseverance. While this has served me well it does present significant challenges to many organisations. It's un-trainable, you either have it or you haven't. The implication for business is that they are reliant on finding, and keeping talented people who can sell, which is far from ideal.

The ways businesses have addressed this, as Carlos describes, has largely been unsatisfactory. The prevalent approach to sales has not helped the buyer or the seller. This is all the more surprising as the problems and frustrations businesses face in their sales activities are a source of endless distraction. Responding to these sales challenges requires a comprehensive joined up plan but this is rarely done. Instead, a series of ad hoc initiatives are tried, but never deliver the required long-term benefits.

To compound matters, globalisation has somewhat forced the issue, as businesses have had to re-evaluate how they sell and engage with clients. The implications of not recognising and adapting to this are great as new competing products arrive daily to steal valuable customers. A new approach to sales has seen a switch in focus from selling to helping or educating. The hard sell is under pressure; the customers don't like it, and increased regulation makes it harder to employ.

The PILOT method described in this book is essential for those seeking to develop a professional effective sales model. It has ignored the noise and focused on the fundamental issues in a practical way. Building a plan to create consistency and predictability does however need an investment of time and resources, but the benefits in doing so are numerous, including; a thriving business and a happy workforce. Be sure to read with pen in hand!

Reading this book you will find it hard to defend the view that salespeople are born, not made. Carlos presents a compelling method that demonstrates, using simple strategies, how to position yourself at the top of your peers.

I hope that The Sales Plan will become standard reading for business owners, directors and managers, helping them clear much of the ambiguity and fog that surround sales and, by using a structured process, produce consistent and predictable results. Apply what you learn to make positive changes to your organisation.

Jim Mellon
Investor & Entrepreneur

Introduction

Things were not looking good. Having left a well-paid job in London to set up as a business coach, I sat in my new office, drumming my fingers on my new desk wondering where all my new clients were. This was not what I expected. With my background in business and investment surely I'd be in high demand.

Ironically the few clients I had worked with all had similar problems to me. They were struggling to build a pipeline of new business. Their experiences were the inspiration for this simple, comprehensive and systemised approach to building an effective sales pipeline and successfully converting it into business success. Sales is a problem of epidemic proportions. Few businesses manage to make their sales work since it would appear that to be successful, you have to be a supercharged, thick-skinned selling machine pitching to anyone and everyone.

It is a consistent and common problem, one which goes to the heart of the economy. Many businesses are the result of an individual, a good idea and ambition. However, other important skills like planning, management and systems and processes are not widely taught. The result is often painful to see. Hardworking, well-intentioned entrepreneurs trapped in a cycle of stress, wasted time and long hours as they try to win new clients and look after current ones. I experienced the same in the City where, the approach to sales was no more sophisticated than anywhere else. The alarming conclusion was sales, or business development to give it its more palatable title, is a grey area with little in the way of structure or accountability.

Somewhere along the evolutionary business path, owners and senior management decided not to be professional in the way they address sales. This is strange given that they are all too aware of the importance of growing their client bases. The reasons for this disconnect I could only guess at. Perhaps it is because of our relationship and experience of 'sales and selling'?

Having spoken to hundreds of business owners there was no doubt in my mind that there needed to be a simple and accessible method to enable companies to become much more effective in their selling. One which dispenses with the need for hyperactive, macho, sales gods, trying anything to shift product to anyone who will listen.

So I set out to find a solution which would help businesses build robust and dynamic sales functions and produce consistent and predictable results. I immersed myself in all things related to selling, marketing, customer service and systems and processes. But, with so much information on these subjects out there, I quickly became engulfed in an academic haze, with little of it understandable, coherent or relevant. My aim was to take this information and produce a practical guide.

The solution is called the PILOT method. PILOT is designed to navigate you through the five key subjects needed to build a successful business development process. It strips out the noise and focuses on the key elements of good selling and breaks them down into the main ingredients needed to be effective. A big influence in developing the process has been the Pareto principle or the 80/20 rule. This states that, usually, 80% of the results come from 20% of the causes. So some of the ideas in this book may appear too simple, but there is a fine line between a practical, usable method and a complex one which invariably leads to inactivity.

Conventional wisdom suggests that being good at sales requires a significant investment of time, effort, self-confidence and a killer instinct to close the sale. However, I learned that to go from a zero skill-level to being highly effective takes a few simple but fundamental steps. The same is true for associated areas like account management, where strategies and techniques are rarely executed in a coherent and practical way.

Similarly, a five minute online search into the world of inbound marketing is likely to leave you dazed and confused. Where do you start? There are plenty of 'experts' willing to show you, for a monthly fee, how to get to the top of Google rankings or double your leads online. Indeed it's conceivable the reason so few businesses have embraced business development is because, confused by the numerous implausible options, they choose to do nothing, a classic lose-lose result.

This book is designed to maximise your effectiveness for minimum time and effort. An overriding theme is 'activity is king'. No matter how skilful you are at 'closing' or overcoming objections, unless you are out there meeting potential clients or finding new ones then none of that matters. So don't worry about your skills as improvement will come over time. Instead focus on building your sales pipelines.

Rather than starting with currently accepted sales practice I went back to first principles, principles that correct the mistake many business owners make of concentrating on the various elements of sales in isolation. For example, learning great sales skills without having a clear understanding of your target market will only get you so far. Or producing leads without looking after your existing clients is another sure-fire way to create problems. At this model's core is the belief that business development need not be complicated. Its success lays in the co-ordination of simple ideas that will enable you to follow the method in a clear and practical way.

The Sales Plan covers selling from start to finish and is therefore wide ranging. Within the book are a number of separate processes. At the risk of confusing you before you start, I will briefly summarise them so you are clear what role each plays.

- The PILOT method is the whole programme and covers all the key elements involved in selling, from business strategy to sales management.

Within the PILOT method sit two further methods/tools.

- The MATCH sales system deals with how sales meetings are conducted. It is covered within the lead conversion stage of the PILOT method.

- The MAP tool is a way to map out your systems and processes in a visual way. It comprises three sections: Model, Articulate and Performance. It can be used for all standard business development activities to give consistency, predictability and aid management.

So get ready to start building an effective and professional sales and business development plan, one which will make your business much more fulfilling to run and increase its value and sales. If you have any comments or suggestions please contact me through the website below and I will endeavour to respond. Also make sure to access the additional resources at www.thesalesplan.co.uk.

Carlos Horner

Part 1: Background

The (second) oldest profession in the world

The mere mention of the words sales or salesman conjures a clear image, and it's rarely a good one. The industry has a bad name. It's a truism that we like to buy but we don't like to be sold to. The inevitable element of pressure is unattractive. Often the first sign of it is enough to spook the buyer, who can turn down the right solution just because of the way it was sold.

Business has helped create this unfortunate atmosphere. Ambitious sales targets have fostered an environment where mis-selling is common. Strangely, selling has not been given the importance it deserves. The fundamental job of a salesperson has been demoted to someone whose performance is measured solely by the business they close rather than as a valuable "matcher" of product and client. Sales management has been equally neglected, with few firms embracing coaching, training and development programmes.

Organisations addressing their sales issues typically do so in piecemeal fashion which produces limited success. Relatively few understand that sales are the final piece in a co-ordinated strategy - the result of having clarity on your market, your message and the value you bring.

The business environment is changing at such a pace it's likely that the traditional sales model will be gone forever, replaced by a more structured and scientific approach used by many of the world's top companies. For newer-sales focused businesses the change will be unnoticed. For older ones it could be a pivotal point in their journey.

Un-natural born sellers

Pushy. Domineering. Lying. Slimy. Aggressive. Just a few of the colourful adjectives used to describe salespeople. Are these characteristics accurate? And where has all this negativity come from? Is it because most salespeople *are* like that? From the snake oil salesmen of the Wild West, to the unwelcome telephone intrusion of today's scripted PPI-type selling, there's a lot to back up this stereotype. Is this negativity also a result of the discomfort people feel about being sold to, especially if it's something they don't need, so they demonise the person doing the selling? Either way, it helps to explain why the job of selling has not achieved the important and respected role it deserves. Surely, we should be focusing on the positive features of professional salespeople? Enthusiasm. Empathy. Knowledge. After all, knowing how to sell is a basic requirement for any enterprise.

In the Introduction I referred to the gap between what a professional sales operation should be compared to the reality of how most small and midsized companies actually operate.

Sadly, many don't approach their sales in the same way they address, say, product development or financial matters. This seems to be based on two fundamental issues. First, the view that selling is in some way not a respectable line of work. And second, some major misconceptions about what constitutes good selling practice.

A dislike of selling seems to be a uniquely British thing. The unfortunate stereotypes apply whether it's used cars or luxury goods being sold. At one time sales was done in a gentlemanly fashion, with deals done at clubs or on the golf course. Over a relatively short period of time it became a high-pressure business with an emphasis on getting the 'close'. It is therefore easy to see how selling has been much maligned by the consumer.

The impact of this is significant. Everything to do with increasing clients, or extending existing relationships, is clouded by paranoia about not being seen to be 'selling'. This can reduce the whole process of business development to farce, making meaningful sales conversations difficult at best and impossible at worst. You could argue that only the British would suffer from this insecurity.

A dysfunctional model

The true purpose of the sales role has been hijacked in the ultracompetitive, short-term, modern world. A sales transaction should be ethical, professional and valuable for both the customer and the seller. Good salespeople must match buyer needs and wants with their product or service, and be content when there is no fit and then no sale.

Unfortunately, rather than recognising the public's dislike and then creating a more palatable approach, the pressured approach has stuck. It is embedded. You only need to look at sales training where overcoming objections is compared to a battle, with one side winning over the other. This is exacerbated by not having a clearly defined target market – making the ability to overcome objections central to closing the sale.

Winning the right clients is much more valuable as you create happy customers who are more likely to make repeat purchases and refer you to their contacts. A worrying by-product of incentivising predominately on sales numbers is the inevitability that a proportion of the sales will not be in the buyer's best interests.

The market seems in this sense to favour the seller. It's even enshrined in law, "let the buyer beware". However, this is a poor concept as it gives the seller carte blanche to do anything they want, while putting the onus on the buyer to ensure the transaction is right for them. The recent spate of large-scale mis-selling scandals should be enough to show us that something is not right. Nowhere is this more apparent than in the financial services industry. The result is an erosion of trust which has serious implications for the public who, in a sector where trust is paramount, may have delayed addressing important issues on pensions, investments and savings.

The emphasis therefore, must be on providing a product that a client needs, not simply wrangling another sale by any means. Selling things to people who don't really need or want them is not only morally wrong, it's a bad idea from a long-term business point of view.

By not selling correctly or ethically you are unlikely to receive great feedback or recommendations from customers who didn't need what you sold them. In the past there was less chance of discovering if customers were unhappy with what they've been sold. Now, thanks to the internet, feedback has become the norm. Restaurants, hotels and venues regularly receive feedback through online sites such as TripAdvisor, making it easy for customers to share views and experiences and, importantly, make informed choices. Peer-to-peer feedback is extremely powerful.

> *"A-B-C, Always Be Closing"*
> Blake, Glengarry Glen Ross

The subject of customer ratings is starting to grow exponentially as the voice of the consumer is finally increasing in visibility. As the feedback becomes more relevant and reliable, there is no reason to believe that it won't become the major influence in the buying process. This is good news for businesses that are providing an outstanding product or service but not so good for those who aren't.

Another obvious reason not to win the wrong customers is the unwanted extra work they inevitably bring. Salesmen may be high-fiving when they sign up a non-target customer, but the delivery team won't as they're the ones who will need to satisfy expectations. The 'wrong customer' is unlikely to become a long-term repeat asset to a business. In the short-term, maybe that's not a problem, after all a sale is a sale!

However, from a cost of acquisition point of view, this strategy will not necessarily show them to be an attractive client.

Impossible to manage

If you have ever seen Alex Baldwin in the Oscar nominated 1992 film, *Glengarry Glen Ross*, you will see a version of what most people think sales management is all about. Lots of testosterone, chest beating and pseudo-motivational talks. For the typical sales manager it's a never-ending cycle of trying, and often failing, to get the team to perform.

Sales teams invariably comprise people with vastly varying abilities. Some are self-starters, with an entrepreneurial approach, who often do well. Then there are the midrange performers who do just enough but can't raise the bar. Finally, there are those who simply can't hack it, leading either to a revolving door of recruits or worse, failing salespeople retained in the company. With limited systems and processes in place, management is a minefield as it's hard to hold staff accountable. I have witnessed countless sales meetings where updates such as *"we had a great meeting with Bob"* or *"he is definitely going to do something, but not sure when"* are given. This feedback is largely meaningless, yet it's incredible how this form of accountability is the accepted norm.

Central to many of these challenges is the fact that so many salespeople have their own individual ways of working. Some find clients through networking, some through referrals while some give free demos. Others seek to close the sale after the first meeting. Some spend time extensively researching new accounts. Others cold call. With all these different tactics it's impossible to work out exactly who's doing what, who's doing well and what's working.

Many companies have good relationships with their clients, especially their long-term ones. However, attempting to increase client spend is a different ball game altogether. There's often a reluctance to sell to current customers at a risk of upsetting the status quo. Whereas the mind-set should be 'what we do makes a positive difference to our clients and we could be doing so much more to support them'. Amazingly, this filters through into many sales plans, that fail to separate growth targets from new and existing accounts, making day-to-day activity unfocused and accountability difficult.

Salespeople not selling. Surely not? But it's true! What percentage of a typical day are salespeople actually engaged in selling? Probably much less than you think – and much less than it should be. As with any role, salespeople are vulnerable to a number of distractions. Admin, social media or personal matters. Remarkably, some don't even like the selling elements of their job and will do anything to avoid doing them. Speaking to existing customers or industry contacts are two favourite sales avoidance tactics.

There are some businesses that survive solely through referrals. In many ways this is the pinnacle of a successful business. What could be better than having a fantastic product or service which delights customers so much they can be counted on to provide a steady flow of new leads? An added benefit is referrals have no acquisition costs and are more likely to convert. Such companies have a structured referral method allowing them to calculate the new business they get from their clients and wider network. In reality, this model is rare. Much more common is the passive referral model. This is where nothing is done proactively to create referrals, with companies instead relying on third parties to produce them.

There are a couple of problems with the passive approach, even one which produces plenty of new business. The sales revenue and growth are largely dictated by external forces i.e. clients and wider network, so the business is never in control of its commercial destiny. A false sense of security, an assumption of a stable client base and a constant supply of new leads is dangerous. It also suppresses ambition, avoids the need to learn to sell and only ever works if the referrals match the businesses goals.

Short-term fixes

In a world of increased competition and eroded margins, maintaining the status quo is a dangerous strategy. But in business there is no guide or blueprint of how to grow. And, while "be active" is a mantra that rings in any budding entrepreneur's ears, doing the wrong things can be detrimental.

Failed initiatives cost time and money and can leave the owner none the wiser. There is no end of experts more than happy to take your money in return for advertising, marketing, sales training, CRM solutions, business coaching or networking. In a joined-up framework all these things have a role to play but, critically, not in isolation. Ad hoc activities can give a false sense of security as you feel you are at least doing something.

*"For every complex problem, there is a solution
that is simple, neat, and wrong."*
HL Meneken

Many businesses try networking but, with no quick wins, initial optimism is short-lived. Failure is unsurprising given the lack of preparation. Turning up at the opening of an envelope may seem like time well-spent, but it's not. You should target events where your clients or referral partners will be. Your pitch should be carefully prepared and rehearsed. Most pitches sound the same and don't make the listener want to take any action. Crucial skills such as 'working' a room, asking good questions and engaging new contacts are rarely trained or practiced.

Marketing is another common, but costly, outlay for businesses that seems to have become an acceptable business expense. More often than not there are no integrated initiatives towards defined campaign objectives and therefore no return on investment. PR, glossy brochures, writing blogs or speaking at events are important, but not just for the sake of them. Branding has become a buzzword in recent years, but a carefree attitude to failed marketing initiatives is wrong. Spending money with no visible return is just a waste.

We all need social media, right? So let's get an expert to tweet and write a few blogs. Only costs a few hundred pounds a month to tick that box. Yes, it's important but, again, if done independently without clear expectations what will it realistically achieve?

Sales training is a must for any business serious about selling. A quick search on the web will find hundreds of experts who claim to be able to 'take your business to the next level'.

The difficulty with sales training is much of it is outdated, using 'old school' techniques. Skills that worked in the past are not necessarily relevant in today's changing business environment. Moreover, unless they put it into action, developing your team's sales skills won't bring you more business.

The fact that business development is often unstructured means it's doomed to failure. One-off tactics are rarely part of a plan and success seldom measured. For example, you may task your employees to attend a seminar to develop referral opportunities. The seminar happens and your people attend, but how likely is it to produce leads? What was the aim or next stage? And with whom are you trying to connect? Can you articulate exactly why they should partner with you? It's easy for well-intentioned but poorly thought out ideas to become a financial black hole.

Joined-up selling

In every industry you find omnipresent businesses that have the best clients and are growing fast. Then you have the rest, who fly below the radar, are struggling to grow and have clients who need lots of support. The only difference between them are that the successful ones are on top of their sales game. The others are not.

Putting sales at the heart of your business takes a different mind-set. It's not about viewing it as some dark art based on the skill of the individuals. A more scientific approach should be adopted which enables a level of control of the results. This can only be done when some fundamental business questions are addressed, such as 'what do we do'? and 'who do we do it for?'. Only by understanding your product and market can you create a sales process which is focused, manageable and gives predictability.

A coordinated approach requires you to understand, inside and out, who your target market is and have a uniform approach by following a standard sales system. In doing this you'll enable clear accountability and the ability to understand why a sale was lost or won. Metrics, such as conversion rates, are used to set goals and assess performance. There ought to be a method to create leads and understand the underling numbers, such as how many leads are needed per sale. For existing clients, it's essential to have a documented process to deliver, service and up-sell, aka an account management plan.

> *"Every minute you spend in planning saves 10 minutes in execution; this gives you a 1,000 percent Return on Energy!"*
> Brian Tracy

A principal objective of building an effective sales engine is consistency. Even done badly many sales tactics such as networking, cold calls or referrals can bear fruit. The reason they often fail is down to poor initial results which is disheartening to the participants, who then withdraw. It's vital that all activity is executed well and makes sense strategically. Using networking as an example; you may have done your prep, have a great pitch and engage with loads of people but still ultimately fail, simply because it's the wrong event.

Most businesses don't optimise their existing client relationships. Looking after your current clients is a priority. It's easy to fall into the trap of thinking that clients are happy because they don't leave, but that's hardly an objective measure. There is sometimes a reluctance to bother clients, especially if there is a chance the response may be negative. This is backwards thinking. Feedback allows the shaping and improving of services. Any complaint is a potential opportunity for improvement.

Here today gone tomorrow

We live in exciting times. There's no doubt about it. Business is changing fast. Last year's technology is already outdated. Start-ups can go from zero to multimillion-pound valuations in a matter of months. Traditional marketing strategies are being cast aside. The High Street has been decimated, with some of the biggest retailers in the world having almost no physical presence. Globalisation, technological advances and new sales methods have enabled disrupter business models, once seen as too niche, to profoundly affect how we live and work.

Technology has had a seismic effect on how organisations sell and connect better with their clients. Social media and the Internet have helped companies to provide faster, more valuable information and support to their customers at little extra cost. A new online sales model has emerged, one which flies in the face of conventional selling, and it's all about information transfer. Essentially, give the prospects as much information as they need to make an informed decision. In stark contrast to the traditional model, where your Intellectual Property is closely guarded and certainly not for public consumption.

The one constant is change, and change at an increasing rate. Unlike previous times, dealing and adapting to change is now a never ending job. It appears there are two types of business emerging. Those which organically embrace and adapt and those which take their market positions for granted and ignore change. A business open to innovation stands a much better chance of succeeding. Given the current rate of development, it's hard to see how traditional businesses that have not repositioned, or stubbornly refuse to, will survive.

Summary

The whole issue of how businesses address selling is complex and there is something of a revolution taking place. For new ventures, embracing the online model is second nature. For older businesses it's an unknown.

The promotion of sales to a central position in any organisation is paramount. In the past this has not been the case. Turning sales from a cottage industry, into a professional business division requires structure, measurement, accountability and, above all, a new mind-set.

Survival of the fittest in business refers to the harsh reality of competitive markets. In the modern context it is not so much about being the fittest, it has more to do with adaptability. Companies that have adapted to market and technological evolution are the ones experiencing growth.

The primitive approach to selling is being replaced by a more nurturing one which enables the buyer, with support from the seller, to discover more about their own problems and the relevance of the seller's proposition. This new selling model focuses on supporting prospects through their own decision-making, and engaging them with collateral to make the process less pressured. This moves away from the sell-at-any-cost thinking.

For organisations seeking to address the question of sales a comprehensive process of planning and implementation is needed to build a strategy that goes to the heart of what they do. Businesses need to be structured so that sales is given the prominence it needs and deserves, with appropriate time and resources assigned.

Most organisations know that sales is important, but simply don't know what to do about it. This is why I developed the PILOT method. PILOT addresses the five key interconnected sales strategies needed to build a highly effective sales engine. One which can generate new leads, close more business, and keep valuable long-term clients.

Key Takeaways

- ✓ Building sales pipelines is a constant challenge

- ✓ Changes in the global marketplace and technology are impacting everyone

- ✓ Selling to an undefined target market is the norm but hugely inefficient

- ✓ Sales is not viewed as a serious profession

- ✓ Traditional selling is focused on individual ability rather than systems and processes

- ✓ Initiatives to solve sales issues are tactical rather than strategic or holistic

- ✓ The sales engagement has changed radically over the past few years

Part 2: The solution

The PILOT Method

Businesses seeking to improve their sales performance are faced with a conundrum - where do they go to? The world of business support is vast. Every Tom, Dick and Harry will be more than happy to show you how you can easily grow your business by training your sales team or buying an all singing all dancing CRM (client relationship management) system. Unfortunately, many of these 'solutions' won't, in themselves, fix the problems. They usually represent an aspect of a larger ecosystem that's needed to grow your business.

The only long-term solution is to consider your business growth in a holistic way, with the elements we have examined above, and others, playing important roles in a wider plan. These need to be integrated into a dedicated system and process so that activity within your business development plan is defined and consistent. This is fundamental to management, to accountability and, ultimately, to successfully scaling your venture.

I have seen many companies failing in their sales activities. Thankfully I've also come across a few that do understand the importance of sales and have built models that put sales at the heart of their enterprise. While much of what is needed to succeed is simple in concept, significant effort is needed to embed this into entrenched businesses practices.

The PILOT method provides a framework for organisations to take and map onto their business, giving them a model and, crucially, a process to measure success and continually improve. The five consecutive stages in the PILOT method are: P for Positioning, I for Interest, L for Lead conversion, O for Ongoing and T for Track.

1 - POSITIONING: Understanding your business, products and client base

A common problem for both professional and amateur sales teams is not looking at the bigger picture. It's all well and good having salespeople hitting the phones, or networking like crazy, but how are they distinguishing between good and bad prospects? This and many other issues are addressed in *Positioning*. This first step is about understanding your product, your market and your clients in great detail. With this information you can focus your sales and marketing efforts, making the whole process of winning new business and expanding your existing client base dynamic and powerful.

2 - INTEREST: Create a full pipeline of new leads

With clarity about your target audience and strategy, the focus then shifts to being able to have a consistent pipeline of new leads. Finding prospects is the lifeblood of any business development strategy. Any successful salesperson will tell you that prospecting or lead generation is the key to success. Without a pipeline there is no next stage as, quite simply, you'll have no one to sell to. A process driven approach gives consistency and avoids the all too common 'feast or famine' scenarios that can make running a business so stressful.

3 – LEAD CONVERSION: Sell simply and confidently

Closing the sale. What is the best way for your potential or existing clients to come to a buying decision? This section looks at both systems and skills. There are hundreds of books written on sales, some great, some not so great and some downright damaging – but almost all are long-winded and impractical.

The simple job of selling has been around in some form since man first decided to barter or trade, but over time has become overcomplicated and invariably poorly executed. The MATCH method (covered in detail later) focuses on the most important parts of the sales conversation to get you and your team performing right across-the-board.

4 - ONGOING: Turn your clients into loyal long term fans who help you grow your business

Arguably the most important part of any enterprise is looking after current customers. If you don't, you simply don't have a business! In Step 4 we look at how to create loyal, long-term customers who value your service, are repeat buyers and, critically, become advocates for your business by supporting you with recommendations and referrals.

5 -TRACK: Measure, adapt and improve

Finding, winning and growing clients is all well and good, but unless your plan lives and breathes it will remain a plan going nowhere. In step five, *Track*, we look at turning the plan into a well organised, workable set of weekly activities using metrics to measure performance and accountability.

The five-step PILOT process is simple and intuitive. By reading, digesting and acting on what you learn from each stage you will be well on your way to developing a business that can consistently find and win new clients and grow accounts.

Step One. **POSITIONING**

In the 1991 film *Other People's Money* there's a scene where Danny De Vito is scolding a management team for having a flawed business strategy. The analogy he uses is the horsewhip. His argument is that the last horsewhip produced was the best ever. Its production, colour, quality, and finish were all perfect. However, there was one serious problem. The car had been invented, which essentially marked the end for the horse drawn carriage and therefore the horsewhip!

Many organisations fail to think strategically. This can result in mistaken ideas such as "if we provide excellent products and services, it will be enough". It won't. You must ensure that your business addresses a clear problem or gap in the market. By understanding your position in the market you can develop effective strategies to support your business development. If you don't you create an environment where the 'busy fool' thrives and excessive amounts of time and effort are lost chasing the wrong customers.

Strategic planning is an alien concept to many business owners, which is unfortunate as it's fundamental to growth.

However, there is a practical way into the subject through a set of straightforward questions which together form the basis of any sound business model.

The clarity that comes from this exercise will help ensure that not only will you be 'fishing in the right pond' but you will also be attractive to your target market by using the 'right bait'. It will help you to develop the most effective ways of finding and winning new clients and develop compelling marketing that will resonate with your target audiences through your pitches, websites and sales literature.

Q. What do you do?

There has been a tendency to get clever with job titles in recent years. For example, a Window Cleaner becomes Transparency Enhancement Facilitator; a Paperboy is a Media Distribution Officer; and a Dustbin Man a Refuse Disposal Operative. While long-winded names may sound important they don't, unfortunately, make it any more interesting for your prospect. And it's missing the point. It's not what you say you are that people are interested in, it's the problems you solve for them that matters.

Much of conventional selling practice is first about convincing your clients how great you are, explaining what you do better than the competition, and then pushing the features of whatever it is you're selling. This method still exists but is becoming increasingly ineffective. Prospects have become bored and immune to this inward-looking approach, as it makes everyone appear like sales clones, which in turn gives it no credibility.

The newer selling methodology is to make the 'conversation' about the client's problems rather than the features of the product or service. This approach is based on basic human psychology. You switch the emphasis of the sales message from the seller to the buyer. This simple but clever adjustment means prospects are more likely to engage as the subject is directly relevant to them.

> *"People don't want to buy a quarter-inch drill.*
> *They want a quarter-inch hole"*
> Theodore Levitt

This may seem like a minor shift, but it requires organisations to fully reposition their whole selling strategy, including all the supporting parts that make up their marketing communications. From press relations, advertising campaigns and sales literature to websites and social media, the language used must be adjusted to become client centric. The goal is to understand and address your clients' specific business issues and then provide an appropriate solution. After many years of leading with features and benefits this will inevitably seem alien and be a challenge, but the rewards will be well worth the effort.

Business owners are focused on creating the best product or service possible but rarely is this done with the input of their clients, or at least not in any structured way. Yet those that focus on their clients' needs will better understand how their product addresses specific issues. The best way to discover how you can make your client's life much easier and improve your offering is simply to ask them.

Q. Who do you do it for?

The issues around target markets are some of the most misunderstood. On the one hand, there is an apparent acceptance of how important target markets are. On the other hand, there is little evidence of companies using them, internally or externally, to help with sales and marketing.

In this section we look at why having a clearly defined target market is vital for every business large or small, why so many organisations fail to do this and the implications of not doing so, and highlight some of the ways to identify your target market.

Why are so many businesses reluctant to focus on a specific market? Much of it comes down to a simplistic view that to be successful you need a big market. There seems to be a huge mental challenge to exclude any potential consumer, even though it's impossible to target everyone. Different customers all have their own unique problems and hang out in different places. A generalist can't offer the same levels of understanding and service as a specialist. If you are concerned about reducing the size of your target market, think about it as a starting point. Don't forget that Amazon started as a bookseller, now you can buy virtually anything from them!

There is also a good business reason not to be a generalist. The delivery of the product or service for different types of client in different markets is never the same. This, I think, is responsible for much of the frustration and pressure many business owners feel on a day-to-day basis.

Consider how globalisation has helped the viability of niche businesses. The Internet, combined with cost-effective delivery, means that a niche product, which previously may not have worked in a local market, can now thrive in a global market. At one time, small target markets did indeed mean a likely smaller business, but with new technology a focused target market can create a significant business!

A clear target market enables you to focus your sales and marketing on their challenges. It means crafting messages that connect with your potential clients and is fundamental to the sales process. Being able to articulate the problems a client faces and the ways your solutions help will enable you to engage productively. This positions you as an expert in the field and is more likely to result in customers seeking you out. Equally, addressing a clearly defined market should only attract your preferred audience and be unattractive to less relevant prospects.

Defining your market can be a little confusing. Is it, for example, customer type, location or industry? And how do you know if it's the right one for your business? The following four questions will help you clarify this.

- Who do you enjoy working with?
- Who values what you do?
- Is there capacity in the market?
- Who has the resources to pay for your services?

Many organisations have recognised how the alignment of values between customer and supplier is becoming increasingly important. Working with people you like to create a mutually valuable result is a great objective. You will do a better job, create stronger relationships and customers will be attracted because of your passion. For example, if you're a website designer and love all things creative, working with design-led businesses rather than, say, engineering companies might make more sense as the impact of what you do for them could be much greater.

Finding a group of people who need and value your product or service is fundamental. If you offer website building services you obviously have a huge market, from one-man bands to large ecommerce businesses. Within those groups are companies for whom a website is fundamental to their business. Those are the types of customers you should aim to work with. Look at how saturated the market is for what you do. Clearly, if you are bringing something new to the table then that's one thing, but if your offering is similar to others and there are many other players then you need to think carefully about the best approach. The worst-case situation is being in a crowded market where price becomes the key buying criteria, not a great business strategy.

While it may not be your primary target market, analysing your current client base is a good starting point and will invariably throw up a few surprises. Try to establish;

- Who are the best payers?
- Where do the biggest profit margins come from?
- Who has the lowest client acquisition costs?
- Where are they based – what sector are they in?
- Typical life cycle?
- Who is the buyer/user in the organisation?

To get a broader picture consider what is happening in the wider market and the economic trends affecting your industry. The Internet is a rich source of data for this so look at industry surveys, government data and information from complimentary sectors. Discover what type of customer your competition is targeting: Are you going after the same groups? Or are there perhaps significant differences in the way you present or deliver your solutions? Who are the new entrants into the market, what are their objectives and why?

Having broadly defined your target market, it can now be customer profiled and integrated into your sales and marketing plans.

Business to business:	Geographic location. Size of company. Number of people and sites. Financial (revenue/profit). Industry. Subsector. Niche.
Business to consumer:	Age. Income. Gender. Profession. Education. Family size. Homeowner. Marital status.

Instead of creating a service and finding a market to sell to, new business models are starting with the client problem then building the solution. These companies are laser-focused on their target market and the challenges they face. This enables them to build products to address those issues and market to them effectively.

"There is only one winning strategy. It is to carefully define the target market and direct a superior offering to that target market."
Philip Kotler

It should be clear by now that a poorly defined target market simply creates an environment where sales and marketing strategies are inefficient and ineffective. In targeting a wide market you make connecting with the buyer much harder. Be clear about your targets. Understanding your market ensures that your time, effort and money are not being wasted. You will be able to communicate with them much more effectively and be able to adapt your services to their changing needs. Moreover, you will be seen as an expert in issues that are important to them.

Q. What problem do you fix?

Try to identify a list of important client problems. Some issues will occur more than others. These should then be sorted into baskets of problem-types. For example, in developing sales for midsize enterprises:

Client Problem		Cause
No consistent pipeline of new business	→	No prospecting processes
Not getting in front of enough of the right clients	→	Unclear positioning
Divergence in sales team performance	→	No sales system
Limited up-selling	→	No account management process

Having determined your clients' key problems, you can identify the causes and develop a corresponding list. This exercise is a central part of your business development and should be regularly reviewed and updated.

Completing this section can be tricky as there is a tendency to think, you already know why your clients use you. Unfortunately, it's the wrong way around. A business needs to understand, specifically and directly, from the client, why they use your product or services. Be warned. It's invariably not because of the reasons you assume!

Let's look again at something that many of us do – buying a cup of a coffee. Let's put ourselves into the coffee shop owner's mindset, or of that coffee brand franchise. Does the coffee shop owner assume we buy because; it gives us fuel for the day, makes us feel modern, the banter of the person that serves us or because of the value for money.

As you can see there are any number of possible reasons. To help find out why, here are a few questions to ask your clients:

- Why are you buying it?
- What do you like about it?
- How does it make your life better or easier?
- Is there anything you don't like about it?
- Who uses it?
- What other products or services did you consider?
- How important is this product in solving XYZ problem?

As this is so important, there can be no shortcuts. It is essential that this step is thorough and completed honestly, as the results will directly influence how you attract and engage your clients. It goes to the heart of your sales and marketing messages and how you structure your solution and delivery.

Q. How do you fix it?

The way in which you solve your clients' problems and the presentation of that solution is one of the most important ways to win over a prospect. Done well it will give you much credibility as it shows that you not only understand their challenges, but also have an innovative, memorable and effective way to solve them.

The goal is for the client to leave the meeting with a good understanding of your process, how you specifically solve their issues, how you work with them, how you are different from the competition and the results they can expect.

"If you can't explain it simply, you don't understand it well enough."
Albert Einstein

When it comes to explaining this, there's a tendency to forget the client doesn't have the same level of knowledge and insights as the seller. Also, in reality, the way we think we're coming across always differs from how we are actually being understood. If you can, make a presentation to a business contact and ask them to summarise what they heard. I guarantee it won't be what you thought you presented and wanted them to hear! Imagine how this problem is exacerbated when you have a sales team who all add their own style. The result is an inconsistent and unclear presentation of the solution and a confused prospect. A clear method to describe your approach is indispensable, not only in terms of managing your business but also for your prospects, who need clarity on how you work.

A great way to present a solution is by means of a process or method. *HubSpot* is one of the most successful and influential inbound/digital marketing companies in the world. They help clients generate leads and win new business online. To do this they engage in various techy/geeky activities such as using software to understand individual buyer preferences. On the face of it, it's difficult to explain. Which is why they devised a memorable way to describe what they do and what you get if you work with them. Their process is simply… Attract-Convert-Close-Delight. Referring to online activity, it means: Attract, get someone's attention. Convert: turn them into a lead. Close: close the sale. Delight: nurture and support. It's simple and accurate. Potential clients, suppliers, customers, and their own staff, can easily understand the method, as it's a logical description of what each element comprises. It also has the added benefit of being memorable.

Adopting processes across your whole business, not just in sales, can have other advantages. Michael Gerber writes in his book *The E-Myth*, that businesses should be built on processes with staff trained to carry them out. Not only does this free the owner from the straitjacket of micromanagement, but it can make the venture more valuable, make scaling easier, reduce delivery problems and increase management efficiency.

Q. What's different about you?

No matter how hard they try, mid-sized companies often end up looking and sounding exactly like their competitors. How different can you be if you provide a similar product or service in the same industry? "I'm an architect, I design buildings." "I'm an accountant, I do people's books". Well, there are a number of ways to illustrate your difference. By the end of this section you will have the tools to build your own Unique Selling Proposition and incorporate it across your whole business, not least in your pitch.

Explaining why you do and your successes may seem a little self-indulgent and not very British. However, there are two good reasons why you should. First, it will resonate with people who share your values. Second, and this is rarely done, it brings the human aspect into the equation. The standard response when asked what you do is typically just that. "I'm a tax adviser." Some may add how they do it. "I use corporate structures to reduce tax liability" but very few will tell you why they do what they do.

Imagine you need a medical procedure and are given the choice of who will operate on you. One is a career surgeon who has built a large practice and is now focused on selling-up and retiring. The next became a surgeon because as a child they witnessed a doctor saving the life of a family member. That experience spurred them on to help make a difference by becoming a medical professional. Who would you choose to operate on you? There's no right or wrong answer but you will probably align behind one of them. The point is, the reason 'why' they do what they do, can be an important factor in decision making.

The author, *Simon Sinek*, has brought this idea into the mainstream. His philosophy is that businesses should have their 'why' at the heart of everything. Instead businesses mostly start with 'what' they do then move on to 'how' they do it, neglecting to mention 'why' they do it.

> *"The goal is not to do business with everybody who needs what you have. The goal is to do business with people who believe what you believe."*
> Simon Sinek

Using Apple as an example, Sinek describes their 'why': "With everything we do, we aim to challenge the status quo. We aim to think differently. Our products are user-friendly, beautifully designed, and easy to use. We just happen to make great computers. Want to buy one?" People immediately feel different about this message. Starting with 'why' makes Apple more than just a computer company selling features. It's partly why it has flourished while its competitors have struggled to match its individuality.

In smaller organisations an understanding and belief in the company's purpose is often limited to the owners and senior staff. This inevitably fails to foster a collective feel and sense of purpose but instead develops an 'it's just a job' mentality, which is damaging to both staff morale and productivity. Companies that do succeed in cultivating a group-wide culture, find clients buy from the whole organisation and not just a few people. This is desirable given the growth in connectivity, both socially and professionally. Your staff, whether client facing or not, are all adverts and ambassadors for the company.

One popular and unverifiable story on this, relates to a visit JFK made to NASA headquarters in the 1960s at the height of the space race. He asked a janitor, who was mopping the floor at the time, what his job was. The janitor replied, "I'm helping to put a man on the moon!" The cleaner understood that his role in keeping a technical and scientific environment clean had a direct impact on the success of the whole space mission.

For prospects to feel comfortable entering a commercial arrangement they need to know, like and trust you. Trust is about assessing if they see you as the right person to help solve their issues. For them to get to this position relies on several factors, which we will explore in the *Lead Conversion* section (Step 3 of the PILOT method). A key element is credibility. You've said all the right things. You look the part. But can you deliver? The truth is they will only know the answer if they engage with you and find out for themselves – but given that this is pre-purchase, you need to prove your worth in some other way.

For many this is uncomfortable ground. The idea of selling ourselves as individuals is seen as unattractive, never mind difficult. Since childhood we have been taught not to show off, so telling people about business successes can be unnatural. It's the tone and delivery of how we do this, be it verbal or written, that will determine whether we are seen as boastful or matter of fact and credible. Past achievements may not immediately spring to mind but fear not, everyone has things they can be proud of.

> US based sustainable clothing manufacturer, Patagonia, has the mission statement. "Build the best product, cause no unnecessary harm, use business to inspire and implement solutions to the environmental crisis." Why they do what they do has seen Patagonia make bold decisions about their business practices and products that don't align with its 'purpose'. They famously stopped using conventionally grown cotton in favour of organic. This was a huge decision for them, given it was a significant chunk of their revenue. They also communicated it to their customers through their visible 'why' approach, which strengthened their brand image and increased customer loyalty. Patagonia also contributes a percentage of its profits to environmental charities.

Earlier in this chapter we explored how important a clearly defined target market is. The ability to niche your target market to a micro-niche is also possible for businesses that have a specific offering for that market. Globalisation and technology have made niches easier than ever to create. Website developers are clearly in a crowded space but can, if they wish, focus on a particular sector...hotels for example. This could be niched further by focusing down to independently owned, then further by location and star rating. Niches are attractive because they have fewer competitors, can be more profitable and are easier to market to. Furthermore, being seen as an expert in a particular area or sector will also give you instant credibility and differentiation.

"To be successful you must be unique, you must be so different that if people want what you have, they must come to you to get it."

Walt Disney

Your delivery method is already likely to be different from your competitors, but the way you present your solution is in many ways as important as the solution itself. If you don't make it easy for the customer to understand, you can't blame them for not choosing you.

Awards, industry or work recognition are always worth highlighting as they are essentially a third party approval. These can range from industry specific, national, to local business. They can refer to the company, the team or individuals within the team. Use metrics if they are relevant, i.e. finalist 4 years in row for the small business of the year award.

Past clients, depending on who they are, can also be impressive. If you are a small enterprise and have worked with Apple or Amazon then shout about it! You can also refer to the number of clients. "Over the last 5 years we have worked with over 1000 retail units."

Finally, clearly articulate the results you have achieved for your customers. For a shop fit-out company the result could be 100% on time completions. Or, for sales consultants, workout the extra business you have helped produce for your customers in percentage or monetary terms.

Why should we work with you? It's a great question and often asked directly or indirectly in a new client meeting. The amateur salesperson spews out a list of superlatives, which may or may not be correct but either way are of little interest to the prospect. Developing a unique value proposition is one of the hardest things for a business to do. No matter how hard they try, they end up sounding like the competition which has no credibility. If you can answer this question well it means you have strategically and carefully thought-out your product, client base and business model.

Q. What's the aim?

The guide to business growth through the PILOT method is largely about taking control of your sales by using a framework to build consistency and predictability. This means that, often for the first time, you have the ability to control your growth with a degree of certainty. Your business ambitions therefore need to be addressed.

Many sales plans are done in the informal 'add a bit' to last year's numbers, regardless of whether last year's numbers were even the right ones, let alone looking at key metrics such as profitability by client type. There are plenty of business plan templates which relate goals to the 'how' they will be achieved. Entrepreneur Verne C Harnish has developed a model known as the 'one-page strategic plan', which may be useful when developing your business model and goals. See www.gazelles.com for more information.

> *"A goal properly set is halfway reached."*
> Abraham Lincoln

One of the first issues to work out is where you want your revenue to come from. There is typically a strong focus on new sales and less in terms of account management or up-selling. However, focusing on existing clients is a no-brainer for two main reasons. One, you will get more business from them. And two, they will refer more of their contacts to you. So, when you look at your own growth plans start with your existing clients and work outwards.

Next define exactly what you are measuring. There are some basic metrics, including numbers of new clients, increased client spend, turnover and profitability. Work out what is important to your business, what you would like to achieve and how it fits with your plan. A plan with a 20% growth target is not particularly helpful. On the other hand, growing the business by 20% comprising 25% new business at 20% gross profit, and 80% up-selling at 25% gross profit, gives more clarity and detail. It is also a good reality check to see if the plan is realistic or wishful thinking.

Sales and Marketing Collateral

With your positioning clear, it's time to ensure this is attractively presented to the market and to your team, so that they can be sure to convey the same message. Sales and marketing collateral (brochures, case studies, guides) is vital to support a sales process. It's not just a matter of randomly handing out brochures. It's about incorporating these important documents to support your selling. The specific documents can vary from industry to industry, but there are some standard items that are valuable to any business.

If you have ever been to those early morning networking events, you will undoubtedly have witnessed many examples of unfocused business pitches.

"We are an IT company and provide a wide range of systems and we also do repairs. We work with all types of clients, large or small. We are different because we always put the client first and go the extra mile."

Who is this appealing to? No one! What's different about it? Nothing! It's as if all companies sing from the same hymn sheet when it comes to 'pitching' themselves. They sound alike, are poorly structured, have no call to action and just don't impress.

The starting point for nearly every part of your business development work is contained within *Positioning*. The key questions answered form the basis of your pitch. For all intents and purposes it's the window that enables prospects to decide if they want to learn more. If done well, it will polarise people into those for whom the message resonates, and those who get what you do but don't need it. This is exactly what you are striving for. A poor result is people not getting what you do but still engaging with you – a waste of time all-round.

There's a saying in the start-up world "always be pitching". The logic being that most entrepreneurs have spent a heck of a lot of time pitching until finally they made that all important connection and their business took off. The more you pitch the closer you get to your goal. A good well-structured pitch is important for anyone in business. You only have one chance to make a first impression, so your pitch is that window that will tell someone if it is worth talking to you.

Take a look at the pitch below, it looks remarkably like the work you did in *Positioning*. Those key questions you answered are essentially your pitch. Add some credibility and a call to action and you've cracked it.

What do you do?	Web designer.
Who do you do it for?	Independent dentist chains based in the North of England.
Why should I listen?	We have worked with over 200 practices supporting their growth with online lead generation.
What are their problems?	No new online leads or booking ability.
How do you fix and what's the result?	A 5-stage process that…
Call to action?	A free website review.

This pitch takes your business model and turns it into a well-crafted statement that will have the listener under no doubt what you are about, if you are relevant and how they can learn more.

Hard copy brochures seem to have fallen out of favour as people try to do it all digitally, but they still have a valuable role to play – and the fact that fewer organisations use them makes them stand out more. Smart marketing is about customer engagement. Brochures are an effective way of impressing customers as well as helping generate leads. In sales meetings, whether you like it or not, prospects don't always 'get' what you do as they're often distracted by their own day-to-day priorities. A brochure helps them get post-meeting clarity and stops confusion with other suppliers.

To be an effective support tool, a brochure must clearly and succinctly outline what is on offer, show an understanding of client problems and what your business can do to solve them. Again, use the *Positioning* section for the structure. In addition, you may add testimonials or case studies for extra credibility. You can refer to them at key stages during the sales process, helping you to influence, impress and educate both potential and existing customers.

MicroIT	Bronze £10pm	Silver £25pm	Gold £100pm
Annual service	✓	✓	✓
Helpdesk support	✓	✓	✓
Discount on repairs		✓	✓
Online training manuals			✓
Extended warranty on all parts			✓

A term sheet explains your pricing structure and outlines what customers get for their money. The prospect won't always get the full picture, no matter how well you've presented it. This document should fill in any gaps, so they don't do that themselves, given the risks that creates. There is an unnecessary concern about disclosing prices. I'm not sure why. Your prospects need to know and you need to tell them. Many online companies do the 'what you get and pricing' bit very well. To get an idea look at HubSpot or Active Campaign to see how they present their packages. Clear, concise and simple.

Have you got an underperforming website that doesn't generate leads, is littered with features and benefits, and looks much like your competition? Does it fully engage with the user? Chances are it doesn't. Yet your potential clients are more likely than ever to look at your website at some stage in their decision process. So it's important to get right. We will look at websites in more detail later but you can make them attractive and effective – again largely using the work done in *Positioning*.

In addition to the essential marketing materials to support your business development work, there are many other documents and tools you can create to engage, educate and nurture your prospects, such as:

- Brochures: i.e. 7 mistakes owners make when…
- Infographics showing what working with you looks like
- Case studies
- A guide to how you solve client problems
- Webinars
- Cheat sheets

While the production of these can initially be time-consuming, once created they are an 'evergreen' asset, which you can use time and time again, and build into your sales engagement.

> *"You have to put yourself in your clients' shoes to understand why they are struggling."*
> Aby Garvey

The goal is to ensure that when people look at your organisation, from both inside and out, they see the same clear and attractive picture. A basic requirement of all your materials is to ensure the branding is smart and has the same 'look and feel' and 'tone and style' across all channels. Professional photography is also a must. Dodgy DIY photos do you no favours and give an amateur appearance. Photos should be shot in a unique corporate style that marks you out as friendly and approachable. The same goes for all written material – use the same style, format and fonts throughout, from websites and social media platforms to biographies, backgrounds and brochures. Ensure your company brand is visible, consistent and clear in everything you do.

Summary

The whole question of *Positioning* is strategic in nature and goes to the very heart of your business model. Without it you are just 'hustling'- speaking to everyone and anyone in an attempt to muster interest. This is actually what many organisations actually do in their approach to selling but, by not considering the strategic business questions, they make the process much more difficult. Sales teams suffer by spending inordinate amounts of time pitching to people who are simply never going to become a client. And when they do get in front of a real prospect they can't describe the solution, or themselves, in a unique, dynamic and attractive way.

Developing solutions for a market you know and understand is so much more valuable than trying to be a 'Jack of all trades'. It is also a more cost-effective way to market to your audience, as your campaigns are run on a smaller, more focused scale. You will receive a better return on investment by targeting businesses that may already have an interest in what you do. As your understanding of the challenges your target clients face continues to grow, you can develop and improve your own materials to be even more relevant. The days of mass advertising are numbered. With the Internet and better positioning, you can be super-focused and discover which types of media appeal to your target customers whether it be ads, videos, blogs or podcasts.

Key Takeaways

- ✓ Just being 'busy' selling is not enough

- ✓ Your clients don't buy what you do they buy the problem you solve

- ✓ Become outward looking. Understand your clients' market and challenges. By trying to sell to everyone, you risk appealing to no one

- ✓ How do you work? Many prospects won't buy if they can't clearly see how you are going to help – can you articulate this?

- ✓ Define your 'why' or business purpose. It's vital for your staff to feel part of something tangible and not just a number on the payroll.

- ✓ What is your goal? Without one you have no way of knowing if you are close or miles off course

- ✓ Create a pitch, incorporating your *Positioning* statement, to be used by all staff, sales and non-sales

- ✓ Produce a range of sales and marketing materials to create impact and credibility at relevant points in your sales process

Step Two. INTEREST

The wider aim of the PILOT method is to generate predictable and sustainable sales revenues. Just knowing who your clients are and their challenges is not enough. What is needed next is a sales infrastructure. This means building systems and processes to create consistency and predictability in all your sales activities, from prospecting to up-selling.

> *"Success doesn't come from what you do occasionally;*
> *it comes from what you do consistently."*
> Marie Forleo

The model is based on reducing the variances in results by using a standard uniform approach. The key element in building consistent and predictable revenues is working to systems and processes. There are many reasons why you should have standard methods for your sales activities, including:

1. **Consistent activity.** By identifying the best way to find new customers and close more business you will ensure all involved are doing things proven to work.

2. **Accountability.** Management of the team becomes significantly easier when you have a process in place. Without one you have little knowledge about what they are doing right or wrong and end up relying on top salespeople. This leads to frustration and confusion as others can't replicate this.

3. **Business agility.** You can quickly amend the process to reflect changes in the market, competition or technology. Knowing that this will be implemented by the whole team makes the process powerful.

In this section we will look at building a framework to find new clients and engage with them in a way that gives you the best chance of converting them into a customer. Finding clients, also known as prospecting or lead generation, is based on understanding how your clients buy, and then building a sales process to reflect this. So, in very simple terms, if your target client always asks his accountant for recommendations, it makes sense for you to focus your prospecting to accountants, and not the end user as you might assume.

> *"Keep your sales pipeline full by prospecting continuously. Always have more people to see than you have time to see them."*
> Brian Tracy

Once you've got some interest, how do you best move them along the sales funnel? The answer is largely dependent on how they buy. Do they want the initial contact to be via information you provide, such as, a guide, a book or a free 'health check'? What next? A meeting? A phone call? Or an online demo? The most successful sales organisations have worked out their best method to engage leads, through much iteration.

Central to sales success is finding a constant supply of business opportunities. This is the most important element of business development, but is rarely put into a system and hardly ever managed in a methodical way. Managers seem to have a fixation with the sale, or close, rather than what goes into creating a sale. Unfortunately, this thinking puts the cart before the horse as the sale is a lagging indicator, a measure of the actual result showing the final score of your strategy and efforts. It is the end point of a series of actions. By focusing on the sale, you inadvertently make it very hard to influence the result. However, the leading indicator measures the activities necessary to achieve your goal, for example, the number of new leads called; if you know is takes 30 calls to win a new client then you have some valuable information, essential for management and planning.

The 'cart before the horse' approach to selling is everywhere, even in some more sophisticated sales operations. "You need to sell 20 more widgets this month," should be, "You need to complete 50 calls, ask for 20 referrals and engage with 10 past clients". Another drawback, of only using sales targets, is that it's common for the salesperson to take their "foot off the gas", when they have hit their targets, no matter, if it's the 1st of the month, or the 31st.

A structured approach is much more visible, logical and insightful. It also debunks the myth that selling requires some kind of inherent skill. When nothing is measured, it's easy to see how sales looks like a dark art.

How people buy

The psychology of selling is a complex area. There are many experts on the subject (myself excepted!). For the purposes of a basic, but illustrative approach, we'll use AIDA (Attention, Interest, Desire, Action) to help you understand the stages buyers go through, and create a method that addresses the buyer's needs at each stage of your sales process.

Attention: the product or service must attract the attention of the prospect; it's hard to buy something if you have never heard of it. The attention stage is literally interrupting the buyer from their thoughts: both Facebook ads and sandwich boards do this!

Interest: once you have their attention you have an opportunity to stimulate interest. And interest is always based on what matters to your audience. As we uncovered in the *Positioning* section, if you want to get someone interested don't talk about what *you* do, talk about what *they* do and *their* challenges.

Desire: now you have your audience interested you need to create a desire for what you can do for them. You can, for example, focus on how to address their specific challenges and the implications. Emphasise the attractive outcomes your clients have achieved in working with you.

Action: you've stirred up enough desire to get your prospect thinking about taking action, so there needs to be a way for the prospect to engage with you. This covers a range of options, from booking a free 15 min call to signing up to your next webinar or a free taster session. Whatever the next step, it must be compelling and easy to do.

Whether you use AIDA or not, it's important to recognise that buyers don't simply just buy on a whim. They follow a mental process, and how you address this also depends to some extent on how your market buys. In the past, companies have not taken this on board and instead built a process that suits them rather than the prospect. This is extremely customer-unfriendly and invariably ends with buyers muddling through, not buying at all or worse, ending up with the wrong product.

Building consistency

Central to building a plan for sustainable, repeatable results are systems and processes. The thinking behind this is that you identify best practice. In other words...do what works then build this into a process to be used by everyone involved. There are many benefits in doing this. It makes management much easier, as you will know exactly where everyone is in the process. You can test initiatives with greater visibility and scale your business much more effectively. Crucially, it reduces the reliance on individual skills. This means that your business becomes more valuable as, unlike most small organisations, it's not based on one or two key people.

"Organise around business functions, not people. Build systems within each business function. Let systems run the business and people run the systems. People come and go but the systems remain constant."

Michael Gerber

In this section we will be focusing on two important areas. How to find customers and how to engage and guide them to the 'close'. We will look at the engage and close section first. This is purely for practical purposes, we need to know where we are guiding the prospects to; is it to a meeting, a call or a demo?

Once you have engaged someone in conversation, at say a networking event, you discover they are a potential lead and establish that a meeting would be appropriate - if a meeting is the next stage in your process. So, the two distinct phases are finding people who may be interested, then converting them into a lead.

Lead generation must guide the prospect to the next step. You have many options available here and it's important to design a process that provides the best chance of converting. They vary greatly from business to business. As an example, here's a common 4-step method:

The discovery meeting is the first stage. If they are still interested then they move to a demonstration, where they get to see the product or service in action. Next a quote is sent. Then a follow-up to close, such as a meeting or phone call.

In structuring your own sales process you may feel restricted by convention. For example, the traditional approach for some professional services firms is to offer a free one-hour consultation. The close is done typically at some point after, often via a call. However, there is a danger in following convention especially if it is not particularly effective. You should use the opportunity to explore other methods, being as creative as possible. Could you, for example, do some pre-meeting work with the client, i.e. ask them to fill in a questionnaire to help focus the meeting. Post meeting you may provide some hard or e-copy testimonials to support your case. Then schedule a call to get their decision.

It's notoriously hard to get back in touch with prospects after a meeting. This is either because they are not interested in moving forward or they are consumed with day-to-day work. This means every face-to-face meeting or phone call is extremely valuable. So you must prepare well. Never leave with unanswered questions or an ambiguous next stage.

The Ⓜ-Ⓐ-Ⓟ Method

There are many different interpretations of what systems and processes are. The words seem to be interchangeable. For consistency we will use the following description. A system is the ordered *steps* needed to carry out a task. And the process is the *way* in which you carry out the system. Take a journey to work for example. It involves a walk, a bus and a train – hence the way you get to work is the system. And the process: Leave at 8am. Walk to High Road. Catch 8.15am bus to the station. Catch 8.25am train to Waterloo. Alight at train station, and so on.

There is great power in systems and processes when used together. A system alone will loosely cover steps but can result in great variance in execution. The process ensures consistency by dealing specifically with how each step is done. The design of the system is fundamental to the success as it must achieve the required aims. Both systems and processes should be constantly tweaked and improved, with feedback from the users, to improve results.

When I started out using processes in my own business, I found there to be little on offer to help small enterprises. I had no choice but to create a method myself; hence the MAP method was born. MAP comprises three elements to building your system infrastructure. First, *Model* the system itself in a flowchart format. Next, *Articulate*, create the detail for each step, typically includes scripts and collateral. Finally, *Performance*, identify the Key Performance Indicators (KPIs) at each stage to measure and use for management. The KPI part is essentially what the whole process is built for, and can only work if your business development activities are done in a uniform and consistent way. Once your processes are built you are then just managing the metrics, which means the process is being followed.

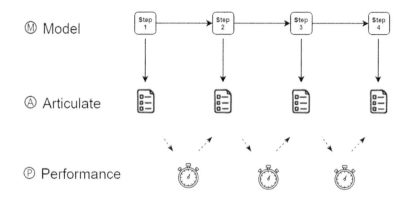

Ⓜ Model

Ⓐ Articulate

Ⓟ Performance

Ⓜ for Model

To illustrate how the MAP method works, let's create a fictional business, MicroIT - a provider of IT security systems to the financial sector. They have a number of lead generation activities in place, from Google Adwords to referrals. It has identified that too many prospects, generated online, are turning out to be unsuitable. It has decided to try to qualify these leads better, before too much time and effort is wasted in meetings. An online interactive scorecard has been built on their website. Potential clients can take a short test to see how compliant their IT systems are. Those that score badly are encouraged to book a short call to go through the results. If still engaged, they move to the meeting stage, and then a proposal sent. At any stage the prospect may disengage. In which case they would move onto another system such as a 'nurture campaign' (we'll explore this later), but for this simple example we will assume they are continuing through to the sale.

This example shows how effective a consistent uniform approach can be. Typical problems of variance in selling, such as going straight to a close or failing to follow up are mitigated. In this case the managers have carefully considered the best steps to get a qualified prospect to become a client. By following this procedure they can harness the power of the whole team and at the same time measure its effectiveness. Equally, by changing the steps, they can quickly see the impact those changes have on performance.

Ⓐ for Articulate

Having outlined the steps, it's now time to create the detail behind each stage, or the best way to carry out each step. We have termed this *Articulate*. Creating suitable and effective supporting collateral is important in avoiding the great divergence different team members bring when engaging with prospects or with other sales activities.

It may seem like semantics, but the creation of compelling scripts is vital. Even minor differences in text can have a profound impact on results. Researchers testing the effect of slight wording variations used by charity workers assessed two options. "Would you be willing to help by making a donation?" Or "Would you be willing to help by making a donation? Every penny will help." Amazingly, just adding "Every penny will help" almost doubled the results, and at no extra cost![1] Don't cobble together your copy, make sure it is well thought out and then test it.

---

[1] Source: Full-Cycle Social Psychology

What you create in the *Articulate* stage varies from process to process. In areas such as email, the collateral will be the email template itself. If you are sending a brochure before a meeting, it will be the brochure. For a face-to-face meeting it could be adherence to your sales process and ensuring you have completed a pre-meeting checklist. However, you design it, the aim is to produce consistent results from anyone following the method.

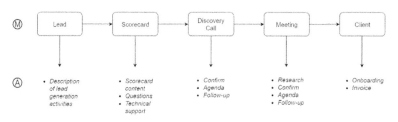

For MicroIT, an online scorecard needs to be built and the relevant questions generated. This is a technical process. There is not much room for variance once it's made. The next stage is to book a discovery call. Within this is a task to 'email the lead to book discovery call'. The email needs to be drafted and filed, or even better automated, so that when the prospect completes the scorecard, an automatic meeting booking email is sent, dependent on the result. Next comes the meeting. Clearly the chances that each meeting will be the same are low. But following a meeting agenda can ensure the same items are covered. This is covered in the MATCH sales system later. Whatever you design at this stage it must be measurable so that you can manage and assess performance.

Ⓟ for Performance

The final section in mapping your processes is to identify what is to be measured, or your Key Performance Indicators. These are fundamental to your work as they can tell you the relative merits of each process and the skill of each team member. Some of the main KPIs will be conversion rates, i.e. the percentage of prospective customers who take a specific action you want, such as those who take the scorecard, book a meeting or become a client. In terms of sales management, KPIs are used to ensure the team members are following the systems, so one KPI could be 'sales scripts followed', another 'networking events attended'. It is important to be clear about what you want to measure and what you do with that information. This data could result in a complete change of approach or just minor tweaks.

There are a handful of standard sales KPIs. First are conversion rates. In the example below, the KPIs from the Lead stage to Scorecard step could be, number of leads created and number of scorecards completed. The next stage is Scorecard to Discovery call. Here you would measure the number of people who booked a call after completing a scorecard.

The KPIs are essentially your targets for activity and for improvement. For example, if your Lead to Scorecard completion is running at 10% you may target that figure by changing how you promote the scorecard (i.e. new title or design). The results of those changes will then be reflected in the conversion rates.

The whole system, i.e. leads to clients won, will also have a conversion rate, which can be used to compare against other sales activities such as Referrals or Networking. This data is important in formulating your lead generation strategy.

> *"Not everything that can be counted counts,*
> *and not everything that counts can be counted"*
> Albert Einstein

Another important metric is the number of leads created, as it's the starting point for your sales process. In very simple terms, the more you create the more clients you'll win. It shows the effectiveness of various prospecting strategies, such as networking, referrals or online.

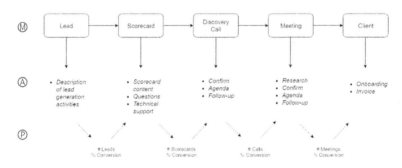

Consider using MAP in your wider business activities. The approach is adaptable to any regular workflow that requires standardising, measuring and managing. It will bring all the same benefits of consistency, accountability and visibility.

Finding customers, AKA lead generation or prospecting

Now you understand how to map and process your sales activities, it's time to turn to what you should specifically be doing to generate and close more leads day-to-day.

There are countless ways to win new business, from mail shots to 'influencer' marketing. In your industry, possibly because of historical reasons, you may rely heavily on one method. For example, a strong relationship with a referral partner who provides a large percentage of new business leads. While you should by no means look at dropping this valuable arrangement, you will benefit most from exploring other opportunities. For example, there are still many businesses that have not yet harnessed the power of the Internet to win more business.

The aim is to assess the various lead generation options and find out which are the most relevant for your business, and then integrate them into your processes. With your work on *Positioning*, this should dramatically improve your prospecting results.

> *You are out of business if you don't have a prospect."*
> ZigZigler

The purpose of prospecting is to move someone who doesn't know you to a position where they are ready to engage. A combination of marketing, advertising and conversations are all available to 'warm-up' the prospect so you can then explore their challenges and how you may be able to solve them.

As you will see throughout the coming section, there are many terms for the various prospecting activities which, unsurprisingly, leave a lot of grey areas. For practical purposes, and to reflect the significant changes in selling over the last few years, we have divided these simply into Inbound and Outbound. In basic terms, Outbound is traditional sales, whereas Inbound uses online techniques to create leads. We will look at each method with a few examples, so you can decide which to use.

Outbound

Outbound, until relatively recently, was the only way selling was done. The approach is now seen as a little clunky, in the way it seeks to generate interest among as many prospects as possible, using the features and benefits of a product or service, but little in the way of targeting. It has been termed "interruptive marketing", in the sense that you are seeking to grab the attention of people who have thus far not indicated any particular interest, but are being shown the promotion anyway, in the hope of convincing them they need whatever's being promoted. Some of the most familiar techniques include:

> **Print and direct mail marketing**: Direct mail has been going for many years and is still going strong. Just check your letterbox each day. It's full of unsolicited free papers and mail shots. Despite the lack of targeting, it's a huge industry as there is a discernible return on investment, albeit small percentage-wise.

> **TV and radio ads**: No one is sure of the effectiveness of TV and radio campaigns but the argument is they subliminally implant suggestions, or brand loyalty. Despite the poor visibility of its return on investment, it's still popular. In its favour, costs have fallen owing to the

growth in the numbers of TV channels, commercial radio stations and online media all competing for revenue.

Cold calls: If you had to choose the one most maligned practice in the sales industry, without doubt, it's the cold call. For some, it's an interesting tool to use, as it does work. The flip side is the public hate them, as do the legislators. So it's a practice that may not be around much longer.

There is no doubt that Outbound works. You can hardly avoid the cold call or the flyers on your doorstep. It's the low conversion to some sort of action that makes many Outbound activities unattractive. It also lacks any level of sophistication in targeting and it can be hard to assess what worked and what didn't. However, many businesses still rely on it as their principal form of lead generation. Those garden furniture companies know that for every ad or flyer they place in a Sunday newspaper they will makes some sales, which enables them to compare against the cost of the ads.

As we will see in the next section, new methods in creating and nurturing leads have had a major impact on the way businesses engage with their target audience. It's apparent that many new businesses built on digital technologies are thriving. So, does outbound still have a valuable role? It undoubtedly does, but it's moved to a more strategic position. So instead of networking to win clients, network to develop relationships with target companies and strategic partners. The idea of selling so early and quickly in a sale is slowly being relegated as it is disliked and its effectiveness is reducing.

Hays recruitment is a FTSE 100 company with a turnover of close to one billion pounds sterling. It was established by legendary recruitment guru Dennis Waxman, who built the foundations of what it is today. Much of the success comes from Waxman's understanding of sales. Specifically, key performance indicators, the importance of consistency and the anatomy of a sale. Hays, like any business, has clear stages for a sales transaction. In Hays, it's the number of calls made per week, CV's requested, 1st interviews, 2nd interviews then hires. The overriding focus is the number of calls made (leading indicators). For every 200 calls made there would be at least one hire (sales). The impact of this on the management and ultimately the success of the business was the realisation that only one thing that mattered –"have you done the calls"? This simple approach was so successful that two Hays executives who subsequently set up their own recruitment firms were also hugely successful. It's not hard to see why. The lessons for others in business are clear; know your numbers, what goes into a sale and the conversion rates.

When it comes to deciding which specific outbound activities to use, think about who's involved. Aside from frontline salespeople, your staff should be, at the very least, ambassadors for your organisation. Given the connectivity of people through social media and wider networks, your staff have enormous potential to help you connect and grow.

You may already have a tried and tested way to win new clients – and this may be improved further by the work done in *Positioning* and mapping out the processes. In this section we will highlight some essential outbound activities (referrals, networking, past-client reengagement, partnerships) that all businesses, regardless of the sector industry or size, should be doing.

Referrals

It's easy to understand why we love business referrals so much. They have a high conversion rate and are free. Contrast this with other prospecting methods, where the trust factor is missing, the prospect has little evidence that you can deliver what you say you can.

Some companies use referrals as their main source of new business. Great! Well yes, and no. It depends how these referrals have come about. There are two ways to get referrals: passively, you wait for the referral, or proactively, where you create a system to produce a consistent stream of leads. If you follow the passive model, you are not really in control of your growth.

"If your clients aren't actively telling their friends about you, maybe your work isn't as great as you think it is."
David Maister

To build a sustainable, predictable pipeline of new prospects, you need to be able to manage all of your prospecting activities. Referrals are no exception. A proactive referral system is where you actively solicit referrals from clients, contacts and referral partners. If you are providing a valuable service and have good client relationships, why wouldn't your clients want to help? In the same way you don't hesitate to tell your friends if you have a great meal at a restaurant.

It's no different in business. Beware though, sharing experiences also holds true for poor customer service.

Build your network

Having an extensive network is an important ingredient in developing a referral process, but also in addressing the wider aim of business growth. Networks can now be cultivated both online and face-to-face. A deep and wide network gives good visibility and a rich source of potential clients and referrers. To grow your network, you need to be active either online, in person or preferably both. You need goals for your activities, like a target to increase the number of LinkedIn contacts or to increase the number of contacts made through networking. Just meeting more people for the sake of it is unfocused and won't work. Meet people who are either well-connected, could be helpful in some way or are a potential client.

Most of us have an idea of the clients we would like to work with. Few have a hit list. Less still have an active plan to contact individuals at those firms. Building a huge list of contacts and then doing nothing with it is pointless. You need to consider how to use that list to help you to grow.

We have grouped the sources of referrals into three main categories. It may be that in your business there are more, but these are three common ones. They are: clients, your network and partnerships. To make them work for you and to start to make a regular flow of leads you need to be active in connecting and nurturing them.

If you use the right structure and tone, you can ask for referrals anywhere and everywhere. Even in a sales meeting where you have failed to win a client, you can still ask them for an introduction to a contact who may be a good fit. This level of activity helps create a constant drip-feed system and not just a series of ad-hoc activities. A referral plan should have metrics on referrals asked for in a given time period with weekly and monthly targets.

Ask Clients

Asking clients for referrals is quite straightforward and should be done at regular points. When you have developed your account management process (which we look at in the *Ongoing* section) you will include the question of referral requests. Making clients feel comfortable with your referral process is clearly paramount. Don't be put off as there are several ways to make the issue of referrals a natural and comfortable experience for you and your clients. First, make it known that you love referrals and that your business is largely based on the goodwill of your clients. This can be done when you first sign up a client and then at intervals through your regular communications. Second, the way you ask for a referral is important. Here's an example:

> *As you know John, our business is referral-based and as such we endeavour to provide fantastic service to our clients, which makes them happy to tell their friends and business contacts about us. Our plans enable us to take on only two new clients each month. From time to time we ask our clients for either a referral to a specific person or just a general request. Would you be happy if we were to ask you in the future? Equally, we know the importance of growing business networks, if you would like us to do the same for you please let me know and we can discuss who you are looking to meet and how we may be able to help.*

The request can be done at a specific meeting, during the year or on a strategic basis. Some clients will be very well-connected and you can leverage this by identifying individuals at target companies where they have a connection. LinkedIn is a great way-in to businesses where you would otherwise struggle. By connecting with your clients on LinkedIn you will gain access to their networks. Remember never to overuse your clients' goodwill.

Try to cultivate the role of a connector, supporting your clients through introductions to key people, such as other clients or business contacts that are useful to them. The referrals you give should be added to your accountability plan and recorded as "referrals given" and the numbers measured.

Referral Partners

In many sectors there are businesses that regularly need to refer their clients to others, i.e. banks or building societies referring to accountants or lawyers. There may be some key referrers specific to your industry. The extent to which they are active in making referrals could make them an important source of new business.

To build a network of referrers you need to identify who they are, engage them, and then manage the relationship. It's the same as finding new clients. In your plan you would need to add referrer as a heading then a target for the number of new referral contacts you would like to make per week, month and year.

When you have some on board it's all about making the relationship work. It's not much use being on the 'books' of 20 referrers if none of them ever give you any work. Even then, don't expect them to be proactive. Each has their own agenda. Some will be supporting you purely because you take them out for a pint or lunch every few months. Others value your product and service, and referring you reflects positively on them. No matter their reason, ensure your relationships are productive and happy.

Networking

The term networking covers a multitude of sins, from structured networking events like BNI (Business Networking International) to informal events such as industry dinners or golf days. I arrived relatively late to the networking scene, having spent many years oblivious to what it was all about. I am now convinced that it is one of the most important things you can do to grow your business.

It's important to make the distinction between structured networking (typically events with the word 'networking' in the title) and other events. For those who have not sampled the delights of structured networking, it's a real eye-opener and has as many fans as it does detractors. Those who have tried and failed will nearly always have been under prepared. You can't just turn up and expect clients to chase you down for a meeting. You need to do your prep. Who's your target market? What are their challenges? And how can you specifically help?

I think the real value in networking comes less from selling and more from building relationships. While structured networking may be worth exploring for your sales team, it is strategic contacts that are of more interest. Try to meet people with whom you can build long-term mutually beneficial relationships. Seek to nurture potential clients, partners or referrers. This could be at social events, industry dinners or anywhere else where you have access to them. While this is a much softer approach, it is still important that you prepare and follow up in a methodical way.

There are countless stories of people who fail at networking, only to pronounce "networking doesn't work for my business". This is largely because they haven't worked out what's involved. Turning up ill-prepared, trying to sell to everyone in the room, having no call to action and then not following up is hardly a recipe for success.

The skills needed in networking are essentially the same as selling. Make the conversation all about the other person. To build relationships you need to be interested in them so you can gain an understanding of their business challenges. If they are your target client you will be able to offer insights into many of the challenges they face. This will reflect positively on you and they will be receptive to future contact. It's entirely natural for your first few events to be nerve-racking, but when you use the softer approach (above), you will find that people are generally open and happy to talk.

If you network once a week, but spend most of the time speaking to your mates, you are probably going to have a nice time but not get anywhere. It's essential to set targets. It may be to speak to one person in particular or to make a range of new connections. Just by setting a target you can dramatically change the effectiveness of your networking. For example, network twice a week and speak to five new people. That's hundreds of new contacts per year and potentially access to thousands of their underlying contacts.

"Networking is the number one unwritten rule of success in business."
Sallie Krawcheck

So, what are you going to do with these new contacts? What is your call to action? For potential clients you can have one process. For strategic referrers another. The follow up is one of the most important tasks in sales. It ranges from adding them to your blog mailing list (with their permission), asking for a meeting, inviting them to your forthcoming seminar or introducing them to one of your contacts who may be a potential client for them. A bare minimum is to connect on LinkedIn.

You can network at "networking" events or any gathering with people you would like to meet such as: seminars, exhibitions or training events. Early morning networking events enable a full day's work after. They are generally open to all industries, typically the smaller end but not always. The value of these events is two-fold. First it enables you to gain a presence in your local market and second, quickly create a large group of new contacts. The downside is they are often filled with professional networkers, multi-level marketers or people dipping their toe in for the first time. Non-networking events such as industry events, awards or exhibitions are often a richer source of contact building. Some organisations use exhibitions as the principal means to get new business, whether as a guest or as an exhibitor.

Set up a plan for your networking by researching the various types of events. Select the most suitable and plan what you would like to achieve and how you will execute it. How many people are you planning to speak to? Identify roles and sectors. Record who is responsible and what the call to action is. Document the process and review regularly. The activity and results should be noted for analysis. Ensure the follow up, whatever it may be, is defined and carried out.

Networking is time-consuming, so it is vital that you do it well. Good prep, execution and a follow up will bring results. Without this you'll get frustrated and probably conclude that "networking doesn't work for me".

Partnerships

> *"Our success has really been based on partnerships from the very beginning."*
> Bill Gates

Partnerships are regarded as one of the most effective ways for you to significantly scale-up your business. They can give you extra credibility, get you into new markets, build brand awareness and add value to your existing clients. Your partner's customers will be inclined to follow their recommendations, giving you great potential to expand your customer base quickly and easily. This process is strategic in nature. It can have game changing results, so consider what would happen if you strike a substantial deal, will you be able to fulfil it?

Partnerships or strategic alliances can take several forms. They can be simple affiliate programs whereby another business introduces clients to you in return for a fee. More fundamental arrangements are collaboration or joint projects. Alliances with trade bodies or other organisations can give you wide exposure to their members and possibly the opportunity to speak at events. A good partner shares the same philosophy, style and corporate culture as you. They can have a matching customer profile without being in competition. Porsche and Armani have the same clients but different offerings. Similarly, corporate and private lawyers are in the same industry but have different customers. Then there are completely unconnected examples that work perfectly – movies and pizzas!

Finding partners and alliances is another form of prospecting. To be successful, consistent activity is required. But be careful, making game-changing new connections should be part of a wider sales strategy, and not the only focus.

Past client re-engagement

A starting point when looking for 'easy wins' is to reconnect with past clients. Depending on the nature of your work you may have also worked with other suppliers on the same project. It's worth reconnecting with them too.

Reaching out to past clients is a no-brainer. There are so many benefits to be gained. First, it's easy to open a dialogue with them. As life is so often about timing, they may again be in the market for what you do. As a previous supplier you'll be in a great position to win the work. More likely you will be nurturing the relationship. Sometimes, the contact has moved. Not a bad thing, as you'll be able to build connections with both the replacement and your original contact, wherever they are now.

Then, once you have made contact, what is the next stage? A call? A meeting? Lunch? Or invitation to an event? Nurturing the lead is all about being helpful and relevant. This may take months or even years, for high-value sales this is perfectly acceptable.

Newer sales methods will never replace the importance of the 'people' element. So get out there and make connections with businesses where you can develop a complementary product, or reconnect with past clients. Rather than networking to sell to people in the room, you should be seeking to nurture new contacts and leave them with the ability to engage in the future.

Inbound Selling

The human part of selling in sales meetings remains important, but the donkey work, in terms of lead generation, and some marketing activities, has been redefined so it's vital to reposition your outbound and inbound strategies to reflect these changes.

Technology has effectively opened the world marketplace to local businesses. The role of the Internet on the sales process has been profound. It is estimated that some 85% of initial searches for products and services happen online and there is no reason to believe this trend will slow.

"Selling to people who actually want to hear from you is more effective than interrupting strangers who don't."
Seth Godin

The principal focus in this section is how to generate qualified leads using digital platforms, and to improve your online profile. Does a web search of your name or company impress? Do you appear in searches and in a range of media – LinkedIn, website, Twitter etc.? When they find you, will they find the relevant information? This is important in gaining your buyer's approval, and their willingness to connect with you. In addition, your online activities of nurturing and supporting leads are not just for new business but can also be used to maintain and build the loyalty of your existing customers.

It's all about providing relevant, valuable information.

There are many different terms given to the process of using the Internet to create leads. Technology is changing quickly so nothing remains in place for long. I won't waste time worrying about correct definitions. The common characteristic is an element of digital i.e. online advertising or search engine optimisation to attract and engage.

It's important to state just how quickly change is happening in the digital and social media world. New products are regularly being launched and existing suppliers strive to make their offerings more relevant. Don't be surprised that if in a year's time Facebook, Twitter or LinkedIn have changed their offerings significantly.

Inbound, as its name suggests is where prospects come to you. For the first time, buyers are now identifying possible suppliers before any contact has been made. This has huge implications for the way selling is done, as it becomes less about sales or closing and more about providing valuable information to attract customers. The online model is about providing as much relevant content as possible, so your client is in a position to decide if you are the right company to engage with. The buyer isn't dependent on the sales team to tell them about the product anymore. They can get answers to their specific questions without having to sift through tons of random information or one-sided sales pitches.

For this to work, the selling organisation must be laser-focused on its target market. The target market, when micro-tuned, gives a buyer persona which is used to target your ideal customers. Without a persona your online ads will go to the wrong people and the results will be poor. Equally, the content you provide must relate to your potential customers. If you are for instance, an architect specialising in the healthcare sector, the content you put out must relate to the issues facing developers (if they are the client), as it is likely to be what they search for.

Consumers prefer the gentle approach

The changing dynamics of sales means that traditional selling, while not finished, needs to be able to compete with highly-visible and adaptable inbound methods or focus on areas where inbound can't work.

Inbound is mutually attractive to buyers and sellers. Customers like it because they learn, in a more helpful and impartial way, about the suitability of the product or service. They also feel less like they are being sold to, which as we have seen can scupper the sale.

Sellers like it because they can produce good quality leads and efficiently nurture their current clients, through their digital content and collateral, which can be used multiple times at no extra cost. The beauty of the online method is it saves you time, as you don't need to be present. People can engage with your videos, blogs and tweets, essentially identifying themselves as potential customers 24/7.

A great benefit of digital marketing is the predictability of results, i.e. leads created. You can identify the costs of winning new clients, the conversion rates, what people like and don't like. This information is much harder to disentangle in traditional prospecting, especially when working without a system. And as you learn more about your target clients, you can create better content that maps even closer to their needs.

If you are not getting the results you expect from your digital strategy, there are a multitude of ways to tweak, such as new Adwords, different social media platforms or changing the formats from say video to blogs. And best of all, the results are visible in real time!

If you do all this properly, you'll be able to create many more qualified sales leads which, because of the nurture process, make them feel less like they are being sold to. This creates a mutually positive environment in which it is possible to have a conversation about whether the product is right for the prospect and indeed whether they are right for you.

Some techno-speak defined

There are many terms which may be new to you, and you'll need to understand them or the next section will get confusing. Here's a quick overview of the key ones.

SEO: Search Engine Optimisation. In layman's terms "Google" your own business to see your online presence and what page you register on. SEO is about trying (through your online strategy) to get your website ranked highly on the list of responses to certain keywords or key phrases. Google likes companies that 'feed' the Internet with information. The more you provide, the higher your ranking. Be warned, it's a complex and ever-changing area.

Content marketing: Selling online requires an ongoing supply of valuable content for your target clients. The online term is called 'content' and includes, blogs, videos, white papers, tools and guides.

Blog: A diary/journal produced by a 'blogger'. Blogs typically cover market-relevant topics. For example, a piece on social media for salespeople may have an expert explaining how to use social media to increase sales and boost their online presence.

Social media: Engage and interact with users online by sharing, receiving and commenting on content. Popular platforms include, Facebook, Twitter, LinkedIn, Instagram, and YouTube. The right ones for you depend on where your customers are.

Funnel: Think about a funnel with your leads being fed in at the top, and customers coming out at the bottom. Buyers go through stages before they will commit, such as awareness and consideration. A funnel addresses these steps as the prospect moves through the process, remembering that not every lead will become a customer.

Online advertising: This is the same as any other advertising except laser-focused on your target client. There are many places to advertise, such as Google or other social media platforms. A great advantage of online advertising is you can analyse literally everything, from the effect of changing a single word in an ad, to changing keywords, to cost per lead or cost per customer.

Lead magnet: Essentially an exchange. Swap an email address for valuable content. For example, download "the top ten mistakes people make at networking events", "take our online quiz" or "download the 5-step guide to...". This is a hugely important tool, as without an email address you have nothing to put into your funnel and no way to nurture. Google also likes websites that engages visitors for SEO purposes.

Keywords: The name for a phrase or word which users enter into a search engine, (aka search queries). For example, if I'm looking for a sports shoe insole, then Google will show the most relevant websites. As a supplier you need to know the exact keywords for your business (the ones your prospects use to find you).

Google Analytics: One of the most common (free) tools to help you assess your website's performance. It will tell you things like how many people visit your website, what web pages they look at and whether they are on a desktop or mobile device. It also gives real-time visibility to any changes made to your website.

Your inbound strategy

If you already have a strategy to produce leads online and have a strong online presence, then great. If not, the aim here is to get you to a position where you can create leads online using a simple strategy. A compelling online profile is also important, as it plays a fundamental role in the prospect's buying decision.

"Your website is your greatest asset. More people view your webpages than anything else."
Amanda Sibley

The world of inbound and digital can be excessively complicated. Many expert consultants, either because it suits their business or because they believe it, insist on building complex strategies, being active daily, advertising everywhere and changing tack constantly. For some this is a sound approach, typically if you are well established in online selling and lead generation. Yet not all businesses need this high-level of sophistication. If you are new, there is an alternative approach.

Many readers who take their first steps into coordinated business growth will be concerned that not only do they need to learn new methods of selling but they need to become digital marketing gurus. Fear not, as with the rest of this book, the philosophy is to become effective, not necessarily excellent. Even if you decide to subcontract this out, it is important that you understand what you are asking of them, and what to expect for your money.

> *"To be successful and grow your business and revenues, you must match the way you market your products with the way your prospects learn about and shop for your products."*
> Brian Halligan

Generating leads online

In a nutshell, digital marketing starts by using several different activities; SEO, content, social media and advertising. These all work together to drive traffic to your website. A proportion of that traffic converts into customers. To get this to work, I've highlighted the following three steps to create a basic inbound process.

1. Identify your target client

In the *Positioning* section we learned about the need to define your target market and understand their challenges. Not only is it fundamental when building an effective business development process, but it is essential for inbound activities. You cannot begin to build a lead generation process without a high-level of detail about who you are targeting.

A buyer persona is a semi-fictional representation of your ideal customer, based on market research and data about current customers. They are used to segment customer types and tailor sales and marketing messages. To build yours, find out:

- What type of content is most likely to generate a response from your prospect?
- Which methods does your ideal customer prefer to engage in when learning about your product?
- What exactly are the problems your customers face and how does your business help them?

2. Create a funnel

First time visitors to your website will know very little about your business and are unlikely to buy straight away. A funnel is a way of nurturing your prospects to the point where they are happy to open a dialogue, or, in some cases, make an immediate purchase. In practice a funnel is a series of pre-designed stages which correspond to your customers buying preferences.

Communication is typically by email and the content should include a variety of formats designed to engage, such as videos, webinars, eBooks, blogs and presentations. This process is known as a lead nurture sequence, which sounds 'techie' but is just a set of contact points. There are several touch points needed for a prospect to buy or to move forward. A well-crafted set of emails should engage, offer value, directly address their business challenges and have a call to action. If, at the end, they have not taken some sort of action, all is not lost as they can drop onto another process in an effort to re-engage them.

As email is the delivery method, the first challenge is to obtain a prospect's email addresses. This is where the lead magnet comes in. This, as the name suggests, is a mechanism created to capture your prospect's email address. Early methods to capture emails, included inducements such as "sign up to our newsletter". However, this is now seen as lazy and buyers are wise to it. Good lead magnets offer something of real value. If you have a clear market and know your prospects' problems, you can create any manner of interesting 'gifts'. These include Scorecards or quizzes, which are very popular at the moment. These online interactive tools focus on client challenges, and provide a score based on their answers. This forms the basis for a follow-up call or further contact.

3. Drive traffic

Businesses were once told that getting loads of visitors to their website was paramount – visits and click-thru's were king! After seeing little increase in new clients, companies began to reassess this view. Because websites were full of features and benefits, inward looking and had a poor call to action, they failed. It was only when the industry cottoned on that visitors needed directing to take action, using lead magnets, did it begin to work.

The main ways to get people to your website is still by SEO and advertising. Ranking highly on search results can be a complex matter, not least because Google decides what a relevant website is and its criteria to determine this changes regularly. SEO is a slow burn, in the sense that you need much online content plus an SEO-friendly website to rank highly – without having to pay for a top 'sponsored' position.

> *"These days, people want to learn before they buy, be educated instead of pitched."*
> Brian Clark

What format should be used to present the content to keep it interesting? Video? Blogs? Webinars? The answer depends on your customer preferences. Do they like in-depth articles or short blogs, where you present a quick idea or challenge? It's not a bad idea to mix them up, so there is something for all tastes. Vlogs, essentially blogs in video form, are certainly worth considering as they are popular and show potential customers the human side to your business, which is important. They also score well for SEO purposes.

Which channels should you use to share your content? LinkedIn? Facebook? Instagram? YouTube? Do some research, find out where your competitors chat and share ideas online. Sharing this content has the added benefit of providing ongoing value to your existing clients who will see your updates. Content can increase its reach dramatically if your contacts share it with their networks. The term 'going viral' comes from posts being shared by thousands if not millions of viewers. Whilst not necessarily in your control, it demonstrates how valuable, interesting, funny or thought-provoking material can spread quickly.

SEO friendly website

Search Engine Optimisation helps Google understand your website better. If it thinks you are a good match, then you will rank at the top of the search results. So Google needs to find your website and determine that it offers something that people are looking for. High-ranking websites get more traffic and are more visible which can significantly reduce your client acquisition costs. Some of the main areas that effect your SEO ranking are:

Content: Google understands words on your website. The more relevant the content, the better your search ranking. Make sure your content matches what people are searching for.

Mobile friendly: As mobile devices have improved more people than ever browse the net on their phones. It's therefore vital that your website works as well, if not better, on a phone.

Website ease of use: Users have little patience when it comes to slow or poorly designed websites. If they don't quickly find what they are looking for, they leave, probably never to return, knowing there are dozens of other sites to view. A good simple-to-use site will encourage the visitor to engage, read on, take action, and at the very least revisit.

Variety of media: To make your content consistently interesting, mix up the formats you use to share your information, i.e. videos, infographics, blogs and vlogs. Also look at varying the length of your updates. Consider longer pieces such as white papers or reports and short punchy blogs.

Contact page: It's vital that potential customers and clients can easily get in touch with you. If they have to trawl through your site to find your contact details they probably won't bother. Amazingly, some websites have no contact information such as a phone number, which does nothing to inspire confidence

Home page meta descriptions: The Google search results page is shown as a list of websites with a brief overview. This overview is called a meta description, and shows a summary of the content and its relevance to the search. These are important because they influence the 'click through'. You can create your own relevant meta descriptions for your website.

Lead magnet: Google likes websites that engage visitors. Lead magnets do!

Image optimisation: Images are key to an attractive website. Use pictures with the wrong format and it could slow down your website and quickly lose you visitors.

Online advertising

The other principal way to get traffic to your site is by advertising. Unlike SEO, which is a longer term strategy, paid advertising can have much quicker results, but can also be costly. Understanding the basics is important for any business.

Online advertising is much more scientific than regular advertising because so much can be done to focus on a market segment such as the location, age or even interests. It's fundamental if you invest in some advertising you are clear about your keywords, or you'll be wasting your money.

There are a number of advertising options available and new ads should be tested on a range of platforms and their performance evaluated. In addition to the advertising giant Google, the market is expanding with Facebook and LinkedIn. The right ones for you are, as you would expect, dependent on the platforms your clients frequent. Once the ad is in front of your prospect you must give them a compelling reason to progress. This is where your lead magnet comes in, as many ads click through to a lead magnet.

Remarketing is also growing in popularity and you may well have unknowingly experienced it. You visit an online shoe shop then leave and go to a news site. While you are browsing the news site you will see ads for the shoe shop you visited earlier (even if you didn't make a purchase). It's unclear how effective retargeting is but in one sense you are starting with a warm lead as they have already shown interest.

The financial barriers to entry are surprisingly low, so campaigns can be assessed versus other competing strategies i.e. conversion rate from Adwords v colds calls. Google analytics will help with this. A/B testing is also useful to fine-tune your materials. This is where you run two mirror campaigns with one single testable difference, such as a different headline. It is not as complex as it appears and certainly worth doing.

Display or Banner Ads are banners advertising a product or service that appear across a page. The banner when clicked can take the visitor from the host website to the advertiser's website or a specific landing page. Display and banner ads work on the basis that target audiences are receptive to messages while they are online for other reasons. For example, a blog on exercise may have banner ads promoting local gyms.

Pay-per-click (PPC) is paying for ads purely on the number of clicks it gets from viewers. No clicks no cost. Google Adwords appear on Google search result pages. These ads appear on the actual list of search results usually near the top, giving the impression they are not promoted or advertising. Advertising on Social media and networking sites such as Facebook or LinkedIn is growing in popularity and may work depending on your business type. These ads are highly targeted, based on a wide range of user preferences, including demographics and location.

Build a compelling online profile

It's vital that businesses capitalise on the fact that most buyers use the net as a fundamental part of their research process. In gaining the trust of your target customers, it's important to have an attractive and credible online presence, as well as being seen to be active within your sector. If your profile shows you give talks, make presentations, write papers and regularly blog, it's not only impressive, it singles you out from your competitors. While seeking to be a thought leader may be a tad ambitious, cultivating an attractive online profile is increasingly important and very achievable.

A compelling LinkedIn profile is essential as Google rates LinkedIn pages highly in search results. Test this by typing in your name and see where your LinkedIn profile comes in. It's important that it matches the image you want your target market to see. It should be ultra-user-friendly, with testimonials, blogs and, crucially, your contact details displayed prominently (the latter often being neglected).

"The true cost of remaining anonymous, then, might be irrelevance"
Eric Schmidt

In relation to a wider general social media strategy, it's good to decide what you want to achieve. It's too easy to get lost down the social media black hole - where you lose many unproductive hours watching videos of dogs surfing or people falling into swimming pools. Be careful not to become one of those ever-present people, who seem to be happy to discuss every element of their business and personal life, no matter how trivial. In terms of commenting on other people's posts and videos, it's important to engage, respond and be supportive – after all it's called social media for a reason.

Summary

The *Interest* stage is the most important part of your selling. Without a lead you can't make a sale. Many salespeople have problems consistently creating leads, resulting in up and down pipelines. Filling your sales funnel requires an ongoing prospecting process.

Buyers are more likely than ever to do their own research online to assess the suitability of one supplier over another, and so the balance of power has shifted. Enlightened firms have taken this on board and created prospect-friendly ways to engage leads, much of which is happily provided for free.

This may seem like information overload but it's unlikely that you will be doing it all yourself, so it's important to have a good overview of what a basic inbound strategy comprises. As always, things change and it's your ability to keep abreast of changes that will greatly influence your success.

Your lead generation activities, both inbound and outbound, need to be carefully structured. When you have decided on your approach, it must be incorporated into your systems with targets assigned and reviewed regularly.

Key takeaways

- ✓ Generating leads is the key to successful selling
- ✓ Consistent activity creates consistent results
- ✓ Build processes and train people to follow them
- ✓ The Internet has changed the way we buy

- ✓ A clearly defined target market is a pre-requisite

- ✓ Create a compelling process to engage potential clients

- ✓ An attractive online profile supports your credibility

Step Three. LEAD CONVERSION

> *"Sales is not about selling anymore, but about building trust and educating."*
> Siva Devaki

Step 3 in the PILOT process is *Lead Conversion*. This is the human interaction component, typically seen towards the end of the sales funnel, where you meet or talk with a prospect to establish if you are going to do business together.

In the introduction we highlighted the many misconceptions there are about sales. The idea that salespeople are born, and the skills required to be successful are based on having the 'gift of the gab' or the ability to sell snow to the Eskimos. Overall, it's a flawed approach and has created a dysfunctional landscape. A lack of development, training and coaching in effective sales techniques has been usurped by a reliance on recruiting 'star performers'. Because so little is done in terms of targeting clients, only a few thick-skinned characters can deal with the daily hard knocks, inevitable with unfocussed selling.

It's ironic that what most of the industry, and the general public, think constitutes good sales practice is so wrong. Rather than trying to just sell people stuff, good selling is about matching needs and solutions. A professional salesperson, with their knowledge and expertise, is invaluable in helping a prospect work out the right solution. This may or may not result in a sale – but long-term it will prove beneficial. The reason this has been so difficult for salespeople, is that they are under pressure to close as many leads as possible. This places a focus on the sale rather than supporting prospects in finding a solution.

The MATCH method is the acronym given to the sales system we have built to provide a clear approach to manage the actual sales conversation. This approach to sales skills focuses on the most important elements needed to succeed. It is by no means intended to be a complex or comprehensive model, covering every scenario, but is again based on the 80/20 rule - doing the few important things well and ignoring those that don't add value.

What is a sales system?

The PILOT method is about using systems and processes to make your business development activities consistent and manageable. The sales skills component is no different. A sales system is merely a process to consistently guide your prospects to a position where they are either happy to buy from you or clear in their reasoning if not. It should be remembered that a sale is not the only positive outcome. A "no" or a "no, not just now" are equally acceptable, as they enable you to definitively classify the lead and either continue to nurture or remove from your funnel.

There are many sales systems out there which mostly cover the same key issues, but are just packaged up differently. In some ways it doesn't matter which system you use as long as the whole team use it and are competent with it. Many of the problems that arise in sales meetings stem from the fact there is no system or method to follow and in not following a system, you are entering the unknown every time you have a sales meeting.

Be suspicious of sales managers who claim to use a sales system, but are in reality paying lip service to it and actually only focusing on results. A true sales system will be documented and evident in the way the sales team is managed. Performance and accountability will be measured against the system. And it will be part of initial new recruit training and ongoing coaching.

Why should you use a sales system?

There are many reasons to use systems in your business. The main benefits in relation to sales are:

- It keeps you in control. You know where you are at any one time and you can improve on it.
- It helps identify and measure what you want to accomplish.
- It gives you an understanding of what is working and what isn't!
- It levels out the great variance of individual performance.
- It capitalises on the expertise of the people involved. When your team understands and trusts the system, they're able to use their knowledge to master and improve it.
- It ensures the sales team are focused on sales activities and not distracted by admin or other non-core work.
- It frees up time, for more important sales leadership activities, such as coaching.

The key components of the sales meeting

You know when you've had a great sales meeting. It's gone like clockwork. The prospect is ready to move forward and everyone's happy. But what was it that actually took place for you and them to get to that position? It's by identifying and understanding these things then putting them into a method that gives you the greatest chance of success.

These are some of the fundamental issues present in most sales meetings:

- Is the prospect a good fit? Securing clients who are not right will become a problem later.
- Do they have the power to buy? Do they need what you do and can they afford it? Commonly referred to as being 'qualified'.
- Can the business solution and method be eloquently and attractively presented?
- Are both sides clear about the aims and objectives of the meeting, and the next stage if appropriate?
- Do they think you are the right person to solve their issues? Are you credible?
- The communication style must be matched to the prospect. If the person you are speaking to likes facts and bullet points, then you need to respond accordingly. Equally if they are focused on the detail and risks involved, your approach needs to address these issues specifically.

An understanding of the fundamental buyer/seller requirements is the background to the MATCH method. A simple sales system designed to consistently and effectively conduct productive sales meetings.

Sales: the three distinct phases

"The amateur salesman sells products; the professional sells solutions to needs and problems."
Stephen R. Covey

A sale can be won or lost, before, during or after a meeting. Having done the hard work of finding a prospect and organising a meeting, it's amazing how many people go into that meeting ill-prepared, without knowing much about the prospect, or indeed what is to be covered. Then commit the cardinal sin of failing to do a simple post-meeting follow up.

To mitigate these basic but common problems, and many others, we divide sales into three separate stages:

Prepare. As its name suggests is the pre-meeting phase and is all about preparation; client research, specific aims and objectives, key questions to ask.

Execute. The sales meeting itself. A clear, logical system to give the best chance of moving the sale forward.

Progress. Post-meeting. Follow up, hand over to delivery and canvas feedback.

Prepare

In nearly every profession there is a huge emphasis on planning and preparation. Airline pilots use an extensive pre-flight checklist. Financial planners complete a multi-point questionnaire. Doctors refer to extensive patient records. Sadly, in sales, much of this preparation is absent. Which results in chaos i.e. trying to impress by excessive ad-libbing and bluffing.

To mitigate this, you need to do your homework and map out the client journey. Research the prospect and your competition. Be an expert in your own product/service. It's natural for a prospect to ask about your fees or competition. It's rare to find salespeople who can respond to this credibly and helpfully while still maintaining interest. Prep is about making sure you don't lose the sale before you start.

Know your prospect

When a salesperson has done the research on a prospect's organisation it comes across as professional and impressive, even though finding this out requires little effort. Creating a checklist of what to look for and where to find it is, in many instances, all that is needed.

First, basic information about the person you're meeting. How long have they been at the firm? Where did they work before? Where did they study? Do they have any connections to your competitors? Have they had any past interactions with your company? Do you have mutual acquaintances?

"Success is where preparation and opportunity meet."
Bobby Unser

Next, the organisation. What is its financial profile? Is it growing, shrinking, are they hiring or firing? Are there employees, other than those you're meeting with, who have connections to you, your business or wider network? Who is the source contact, and what's the contact history?

Where do you find this information? Try LinkedIn and Google as starting points. This task can be 'subbed out' to a colleague using a checklist for efficiency, i.e. use LinkedIn to: 1. Establish intercompany contacts; 2. List previous companies worked at; 3. Cross-reference against your current and past client list.

Develop a question bank

Like much in this book, creating a list of common questions and answers is simple and practical, but not generally adopted in businesses. Great answers to client questions are extremely important as it demonstrates you have a good understanding of your products and client concerns. Poor responses only damage the sale and it's not enough to assume your sales team can do this well.

For example, how confident are you that you, and your team, can answer questions like *"your product is not up to scratch"* or *"you are just too expensive"* with clarity and honesty while converting these potential pitfalls into positives?

With your sales team create a list of the 5-10 (or more) most common client questions. Then formulate the best answers, which will please and impress the prospect. Then practice them until they become second nature. The result should be a standard, attractive, uniform response by all team members.

Talk the talk

One small concession to the much-lauded skill of traditional salespeople is the ability to charm. It's well-known that 'people buy from people' – or to clarify, "people buy from people they like!". Although you can't make someone like you, there are ways to stop people taking a dislike to you. In the sales environment, it's important to be literally 'talking the same language' as your prospect. This requires basic communication skills and an understanding of personality styles.

> *"Understanding people certainly impacts your ability to communicate with others."*
> John C. Maxwell

This is about adapting the way you communicate with the prospect. If you go into extensive detail about what you do and how your product works, but the person you are pitching to does not 'do' detail, they'll feel uncomfortable, which will make your chances of a sale slimmer.

As it's a given that potential clients won't adapt their style to suit yours, you must communicate in a way that makes your prospect feel comfortable. To do this you must understand something about their personality and preferences. Without descending into pseudo-psychological claptrap, there is a relatively simple method to help you to understand people and their behaviours in a practical way.

In 1928, William Moulton Marston developed the DISC model. This model categorised personality into four types: Dominance, Influence, Steadiness and Conscientious. DISC helps to understand people's motivations and priorities in various environments. In turn it helps us to adjust our style and improve how we communicate with them. DISC has a range of applications in management and the sales environment.

Dominance: "D" profiles are all about getting results and quickly. They tend to be dominant, decisive and to the point. They enjoy challenges and thrive on competition. They like to be in control and are not afraid to take risks. However, they may come across as insensitive and impatient, with an apparent lack of empathy. Famous D's include, Simon Cowell, Margaret Thatcher, and Gordon Ramsay.

Influence: "I" profiles are very social, outgoing, optimistic and charming. They are enthusiastic; enjoy having fun and creating a positive environment. They are generally not into detail, fear rejection or loss of influence, and can come across as disorganised and impulsive. Famous I's include, Bill Clinton, Tony Blair, Richard Branson and Oprah Winfrey.

Steadiness: "S" profiles are great team players. They do not like the limelight but are people-orientated. They are often very supportive and dislike conflict, so they focus on collaboration and creating a harmonious environment. They are generally patient and have a calm, methodical approach. Famous S's include, Lady Di, Mother Teresa, and Ghandi.

Conscientious: "C" profiles are focused on quality, detail and accuracy. They can be reserved but are task-orientated. C's are also known as cautious as they always focus on facts, stick to the rules, and are risk averse. They can appear indecisive because of their desire to mitigate any failure, fear criticism and any question of their abilities. Famous C's include, Bill Gates, Stephen Hawking, and Albert Einstein.

In practice people have elements of all four but are skewed towards one or two. So when dealing, for example, with a "D" profile you will need to be to the point, not over-elaborate and demonstrate quickly how your product or service will work. In contrast, when pitching to a "C", you will need to cover each element of your offering in detail and be able to show clearly the risk and reward profile.

An understanding of behavioural styles is invaluable in sales. Not only does it allow you to adapt your communication style to your buyer's, it also helps you make a positive connection in the sales meeting. It's important this is carried over to nonverbal communications i.e. sales and marketing collateral - where the same issues arise.

To become proficient in understanding and utilising the different behavioural types, you will need to build this into your training and coaching. People skilled in this area can identify profile types within minutes. To maximise the impact of your sales activities, assess all client touch points and adjust to incorporate the different personality types.

Prove your credibility

I dislike the term 'elevator pitch'. It reminds me of sitting though dreary networking events with salespeople trying their best to present their business, but invariably breaking every rule of the pitch. Why is the pitch so important? A pitch is simply the answer to the question; what do you do? And for anyone in sales, it's a fundamental part of their job.

Done well, a pitch enables you to demonstrate your credibility, show you understand your client's problems, provides a compelling solution and gives the listener a clear route to engage further. Given that the pitch is so important it is staggering how little effort companies spend in getting their team to present a unified, attractive and robust one. If you think this is overstating the problem, ask your sales team to write down their pitch format and content. Are they consistent, interesting, different, and do they impress?

It's an area that all sales organisations struggle with and as a result end up coming across the same as everyone else. This is because there's a feeling that a compelling and unique pitch is impossible to create, because after all, businesses in the same sector do the same thing don't they? Not true, as we saw in *Positioning*, there are many ways to demonstrate your unique value.

Like all the tools and tactics in this book, no one initiative will revolutionise your business. Having a good pitch is the foundation of how to present your business, either verbally or written, every moment of everyday. Fortunately, the framework for building a compelling and attractive pitch was covered in the *Positioning* section. When complete, it's crucial the whole team is able to consistently present it well.

Know your stuff

Having great certainly about what you do gives your customers and prospects confidence in your ability to help. However, salespeople always struggle when it comes to how they present their offering and typically, there is information overload. This is when the salesperson destroys the sales pitch by over-elaborating, referring to every conceivable bell and whistle the product has. We will look at how the prospect meeting should be structured later, but for now the focus is on knowing all the essentials about your product or solution.

An in-depth knowledge of your product and organisation is a basic requirement of the job, but it's scary how the easiest questions seem to be the hardest to answer - When will it be delivered? Who will be my contact if I sign up? What is your best price? How can I pay? What if I am not happy with the product? I'm interested, what happens now? These are just a few examples of very simple questions you must be able to answer well.

We have looked at developing a question bank for responses to common client questions, but another basic skill of a good salesperson are the questions they ask the prospect. Good questions are the hallmark of good selling as they give clarity on the prospect's true situation. Asking the prospect about themselves shows that you are interested in what they do and value their opinion. Identification and dissemination of the most important questions should be carried out by the sales team and added to and improved with feedback from client meetings.

Third party stories and case studies are a valuable way to illustrate how you have successfully supported other businesses. People like to see what other organisations (or ones they aspire to be like) have done in similar situations. How they solved specific problems, and what the result was. Stories that your prospect can identify with are powerful, showing how a customer like them made, and benefited from, the decision to buy from you. It's why customer reviews on Amazon, Google and Yelp carry such weight. Layer these ideas into your sales process with a selection of third-party stories to cover the most common scenarios which directly, or in parallel, relate to your target audience.

"We worked with a £5m turnover business in the tech space. They were consistently struggling to find new business. The sales team were succeeding some months but failing in others. Many of the leads generated were unsuitable for their business. They heard about the PILOT method through one of their suppliers and as a result came to one of our half-day seminars. They realised that they were making some fundamental sales mistakes. Shortly after they became a client they immediately developed a USP and clear target market. They then had their sales teams trained working to the same (MATCH) system. They now build pipelines of the right type of clients and have a more effective sales team who are easier to hold accountable, and this year looks like their best in terms of sales."

How are you different?

Given that your potential clients will probably be talking to your competitors, it's important to do a competitive analysis and have a plan to address rival products. Just to be clear, this is not about trying to badmouth or steal business; it's still about trying to match the prospect to the right solution and supplier. This may sound counterintuitive but it means that you could actually refer an off-target prospect to one of your competitors. Why, you ask? Three reasons. One, it's the right thing to do as they will be better served by the other provider. Two, in *Positioning*, we learned that winning the wrong type of clients creates future problems. Three, by simply doing the right thing, they will want to help you in return should the opportunity arise.

> *"You can't look at the competition and say you're going to do it better. You have to look at the competition and say you're going to do it differently."*
> Steve Jobs

Understanding the competitor landscape not only helps in the sales conversation but also keeps your business aware of changes and challenges developing in the market. Whilst companies in the same industry may appear similar, there are always differences, no matter how small, such as customer size, levels of support, online offering, pricing or technical expertise. Understanding those differences means you can address them head-on in sales conversations. If they are interested in working with your competition, but are better suited to your business you can deal with this using insightful questions which will lead them to consider if your competitor is indeed the right option.

It's also worth remembering that just because a prospect is a good fit for you, they may still go with a less suitable competitor. This is always a frustration and it's wrong to be flippant, but the reality is 'you win some, you lose some' and sales is about increasing the 'yes's' while accepting there will always be many 'no's'.

Have purpose

The last piece in the Preparation section is about the aims and objectives of the meeting. Since traditional selling is all about activity, it's common to hurtle from one meeting to another without really pre-agreeing the purpose of each meeting. It's standard practice to say "let's grab a coffee". Unfortunately, this creates ambiguity – as the agenda and what happens next are not agreed. If the purpose is not clear, time is wasted, as nearly almost anyone will agree to a coffee, but few will readily book in a sales meeting.

Stating the purpose of the discussion can result in a much more relaxed and open conversation – whether in Starbucks or a boardroom. Explaining how your sales process works can give the buyer clarity and confidence. This avoids the claims that you are misleading them. So, why not explain early on, the way you typically find and work with new clients. This is a simple example, to give you an idea:

"John, would it be helpful if I briefly explain to you the steps we go through with potential clients to decide if there is a good fit... Great, thank you. The first is a discovery call where we spend 30 mins going through the headline issues and we touch on our products. If we both agree it makes sense to meet, we will schedule a meeting with you and possibly your finance director and dig deeper into your challenges."

It's also important to remove the element of pressure, by making clear that at every stage it's possible for either party to decide there isn't a fit and discussions can stop with no obligation. The agenda should be agreed before the meeting and potential outcomes set out. This small tactic has a huge impact in making your sales meetings productive by consistently leading to a clear outcome.

Prep Checklist

To build good preparation into your process, devise a checklist that your salespeople cover before each meeting. This will help them to ensure they are well prepared and will enable you to monitor their performance.

- Purpose and potential outcomes of the meeting agreed?
- Meeting confirmed?
- Pitch prepared?
- Research company/individual?

- Mutual connections?
- Contact history?
- Likely DISC profile?
- Likely competitors for this work and analysis sheet?
- Question bank: questions to ask/likely questions received?
- Third party stories?
- Collateral: brochures, business cards, term sheets, pricing, engagement process etc.

This simple proactive approach gives you the best chance to move the sale forward. It is neither particularly difficult nor time-consuming, but it will ensure that you come across professionally and can articulate the purpose of the meeting.

Building a set of key questions to ask your prospects will help you understand the true picture and illustrate your expertise while making the client feel they are being heard. Having put together credible answers to difficult client questions you will also impress with your comprehensive level of knowledge. Adjusting your communication style will also help with the connection and mitigate the potential for a clash of personalities.

Formally review the preparation process regularly with staff feedback. In addition, Prep should be measured, monitored and included in the sales team's performance as a KPI.

If you fail to prepare then prepare to fail!

EXECUTE

> *"Every sale has five basic obstacles: no need,
> no money, no hurry, no desire, no trust."*
>
> ZigZiglar

We've reached the sales meeting or conversation stage. The prospect will have satisfied much of their buying criteria. They are now interested enough to have a face-to-face meeting. However, even though they may have gone through a similar journey, not all leads are the same, with some more likely to convert than others. This may be due to failures on the seller's side, or because it was simply not meant to be.

Beware the all too common ambiguous meeting outcomes. The prospect says, *"we'll be in touch"* your salesperson translates this into *"great meeting, I expect an order"*, but nothing more is heard. A good sales system should be the framework for every sales meeting. Use it actively as you progress through the meeting. It gives you confidence, puts you in control and removes common problems such as getting side tracked. It also enables you to effectively manage, train and hold staff accountable. A sale can fail in many different areas and it's important to remember that converting every prospect is unrealistic. But by focusing on the key components in the negotiation, you can improve performance considerably.

Connection

Sales is about people, personalities and the extent to which there is a connection. So, the first thing to recognise is the people part of any meeting. It's vital for there to be some compatibility or connection. If they don't trust you or like you, chances are they won't buy from you. The onus is therefore on the salesperson to do what they can, without being disingenuous, to nurture the prospect and build rapport.

Investment/budget

This is a pretty fundamental question. You may have found someone who loves what you do, has a clear need and wants to progress. However, there is a problem; they don't have the money to make it happen. Salespeople commonly get stuck with this type of prospect. Their genuine interest and apparent desire to progress makes the salesperson blind to the fact there is no money to make the purchase. Sometimes they continue to engage with leads with an inadequate or non-existent budget, as they feel the buyer will come back once they do have the funds, with the time invested seen as essential groundwork. This is not unreasonable, but a consistent sales process should create substantial numbers of qualified leads that have a present need and budget to solve an important issue.

> *"The reason it seems that price is all your customers care about is that you haven't given them anything else to care about."*
> Seth Godin

Authority

Does your lead have the power to make the buying decision? Another classic way to waste valuable time, is pitching to a non-decision maker. This is a common problem as eager salespeople can overlook this basic piece of intelligence and believe, mistakenly, that meeting anybody at a target company is a good thing. This belief comes from the idea than the person you meet will have an influence in the buying process. However, this rarely happens. It's hard to sell upwards, as the message you present is always misrepresented, which can cause more damage than good. Getting the right people in the room is fundamental and if they are not available, reschedule the meeting.

Need and desire

Is there a pain point that your product or service can solve? Sometimes your prospects may have a need or want which you may be able to fix. Other times they don't because they are unaware of it, or they may simply not have one. This element is a key step in the sales process. Without a need and a want there is basically no reason for them to do anything.

Time frame

What is your prospect's purchasing timeframe? And does it align with your sales cycle? An understanding of the timing means you can gauge how important it is for the client to fix, expose any blocks to continuing and plan your internal resources accordingly. This also verifies earlier responses, i.e. they say they have an urgent problem, costing lots of money, but when questioned on timings they are in no rush. Further investigation is required.

The MATCH sales system

In response to these ever-present issues we built the MATCH method. MATCH is a 5-step system to enable you to effectively manage the sales meeting. It covers the crucial steps needed to guide your prospect to a logical conclusion, be that a sale, a no or the next stage.

M - Make ready

A - Add credibility

T - Test and qualify

C - Create solution

H - Handover

M. Make ready

This is about setting the scene and ensuring you don't scupper the meeting because of a lack of a connection or, worse, a clash of personalities. There's always going to be small talk in the initial stages of a meeting. Given this, why not prepare what to say or ask? Your research in the *Prep* stage will have undoubtedly uncovered information about mutual connections, contact history or their background, that can be referred to.

We discussed in the last section the benefits of disclosing your process to potential customers. This gives both sides clarity and control, in terms of where the discussions are going and how a mutual withdrawal is allowable. Agreement of the purpose is important at the meeting setup stage or you are at risk of the dreaded "coffee" or "catch up" meeting. If it's a sales meeting and both sides are not agreed then one will surely be caught off guard when it comes to talking about next steps. Clearly stating why you are meeting and the possible outcomes radically changes the dynamic of the meeting.

This should be communicated and agreed at the meeting setup stage, or before via email at some point. Once you've completed the pleasantries, it's time to frame the meeting.

History: Summarise the contact history to date.
Purpose: Agenda and timings.
Outcomes: List possible outcomes.

> *"We have had a few conversations about the new generator for your York plant. You have got most of the technical spec and pricing by now. I think this meeting is really to establish if the R453 is the right product for you and to give you the opportunity to ask any further questions you may have. If it is all good, we will look at an implementation date. If not, we can explore other solutions that may be more suitable. Does that make sense?"*

Once the agenda has been outlined it's important to reach agreement with the prospect so they can add anything specific. The tendency of salespeople to meet anyone who has shown a mild or passing interest, is a great area of inefficiency. Making meetings much more effective requires no "natural born" sales skills, just some professionalism and structured preparation.

A. Add credibility

Given that your prospect has probably sat through countless sales meetings, it is important to impress and stand out from your competition. In the *Positioning* section you largely drafted your own pitch. This should be used here to give your prospect a very clear picture about you, your experience, your credibility and why they should want to work with you. The pitch should never be showboating. Do it in a matter-of-fact but professional way, allowing a smooth transition to the next section "test and qualify".

"Why don't I tell you, very briefly about us, then we can delve into you and your business?"

T. Test and qualify

It's time to get to the nitty-gritty of the meeting, a subject where many salespeople struggle. This is how to conduct sales meetings which are consistently productive. What you are trying to achieve at each meeting depends on where you are in the sale. Some sales meetings are to pitch for the business, others are to progress the sale to the next stage. Every buyer will come into a meeting with different states of readiness to purchase. You have no influence on that, but you can control three key qualification criteria. Do they have a significant problem which they want to fix? Can they afford it? And are they able to make the buying decision?

Clear and present problem. In exploring your prospects issues and challenges, there are several points to establish. First, does the prospect have a problem to solve? From the outside you may clearly see an issue, but don't assume the prospect feels the same way. Your interpretation shouldn't be forced on them. They may think it's not a significant enough issue or they may not yet be aware that it poses a problem. It's essential the salesperson is able to explore and suggest actions if it is important enough for their consideration. An open mind is essential, because they may have different priorities, in which case you must move on and not dwell on something you regard as a fundamental problem.

There is a tendency to rush through the analysis and investigation of client problems, and start selling too early. It's the accepted model. Give as much information about what you do and hope that some of it maps onto their issues. This type of features and benefits selling has little emphasis on qualification. It's largely a numbers game; present to enough people and some will buy. While this is true it is also inefficient and dumbs-down the job of the salesperson.

Question & Listen. A principal objective in the sales meeting should be about qualifying the prospect. Only when this is done can the conversation turn to addressing a solution. This can prove difficult, as the consensus is that a good salesperson must impress by their ability to talk. This approach should actually be reversed. The real ability of a professional salesperson is to get the prospect talking, as they will disclose valuable information relevant to the sale – impossible if the salesperson is in presentation mode. There are several techniques to get your target client talking. The main one is the most straightforward – simply ask them questions!

The Greek philosopher Socrates was famous for posing relevant questions to inspire learning. The logic being that by inspiring his students to ask their own questions they would arrive at the correct answer, or solution, through their own reasoning. This is recognised as a more powerful method of learning, rather than simply being presented with the answer. In the same way, the ability in a sales situation to stimulate prospects into questioning their own challenges helps them to reach their own conclusion as to whether an issue must be resolved or not. This has a far more positive impact on the selling process than merely telling a prospect they have a problem.

As with any skill, practice is required to master this style of questioning. When you have, it will become second nature. You'll be able to get to the nub of the issue in a faster more constructive way. It will also feel very different, in a positive way, for the prospect, who will more than likely, be used to the standard approach of a salesperson talking for most of the meeting. Refer to your question bank and use insightful questions to help the prospect gain greater understanding of their own issues.

Problems are all about perception. One man's problem can be a mere annoyance to another. It's important the salesperson can quantify the problem with the prospect. Put the problem

119

into context and understand what the impact has been. Your questioning, if done well, will get you to a position where a problem has been acknowledged. Next is to find out how it has affected the organisation. If, for example, the problem has taken the company to its lowest sales in three years, has affected the decision to expand into new markets, and reduced pay and bonuses, it would indeed seem an important issue to address.

Learning what has already been done to solve the problem will give useful insights into their thinking and how to best help them. It will show the prospect's appetite for resolving the issue. If they don't want, or feel, the need for your input, move on. If, however, they are aware and have tried to come up with their own fix, it tells you they are serious. The solution they tried will tell you about their attitude to the problem. It will give you an idea into what their budget and tactics might be. In other words, do they want a sticking plaster solution or do they have the funding to deal with the root cause?

"People don't buy for logical reasons, they buy for emotional reasons."
ZigZigler

If you reach this stage, and have satisfied all the previous criteria, it's time to find out if they can afford your solution. Talking about money is one of those subjects people have difficulty with. The professional salesperson should have no issues at all. Any hesitation or uncertainty at this stage undoes all the hard work, and can result in discounting or losing the sale.

Where possible it's important to frame your price against the likely cost of their continuing business challenges. For example, a £50k manufacturing improvement fee sounds expensive. However, if there has been some £500k of inefficiencies identified, then the price appears much more attractive. The financial implication of your service should always be in relation to savings made and the overall result.

The final part of this section is the decision-making process. You can have the best meeting ever, satisfying all the qualification steps, only to learn the person you have presented to, loves what you've proposed, but can't make the final decision without approval from 'the boss'. This could mean the end of the discussion and possibly a lost opportunity. So, ensure in advance that you are meeting with the decision maker before you invest your time. Even if you have already established the decision-making structure, do so again at the meeting.

Test & Qualify, summary key steps

Problem: What are the symptoms?

Impact: Is it a real and significant problem?

Repair: What has been done to fix it?

Funding: What would it cost to fix and is there a budget?

Decision: How are decisions made, who is involved, and what is the time frame?

C. Create solution

Now that you have qualified your prospect to the best of your ability, it's time to discuss the solution. If you think back to the *Positioning* section, you should have created a clear, dynamic and compelling way to show how you help your clients achieve their aims. This should incorporate their challenges, how they are solved using your product and what the lasting result is.

> *"Sell the problem you solve not the product."*
> Unknown

Building a method to address common client problems, makes the solution so much easier to explain. It will also give your prospects the confidence and certainty that you have a clear understanding of their business issues, and have developed a proven solution. This ensures you'll stand out from your competition, who typically have not thought through the pitching of the solution. However, it's more than apparent that without an ideal customer profile, solution development becomes a very difficult process indeed. Different types of customers all have diverse problems and therefore can't be helped in the same way.

For example, PILOT is a 5-step process to build consistent predictable sales. Each of the five steps, solves typical client problem:

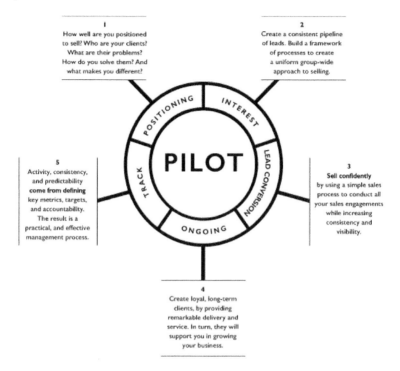

1
How well are you positioned to sell? Who are your clients? What are their problems? How do you solve them? And what makes you different?

2
Create a consistent pipeline of leads. Build a framework of processes to create a uniform group-wide approach to selling.

5
Activity, consistency, and predictability come from defining key metrics, targets, and accountability. The result is a practical, and effective management process.

3
Sell confidently by using a simple sales process to conduct all your sales engagements while increasing consistency and visibility.

4
Create loyal, long-term clients, by providing remarkable delivery and service. In turn, they will support you in growing your business.

POSITIONING · INTEREST · LEAD CONVERSION · ONGOING · TRACK

PILOT

And the ultimate goal of the PILOT method? To generate more sales with consistency and predictability using systems and processes.

This final part of the meeting must flow smoothly. There can be no unanswered questions or doubt in the prospect's mind. The question of what happens next is another potential pitfall. If the buyer is unsure about how the delivery works, it can scupper the sale.

"Significant organisational change requires an investment of time. The Pilot course is delivered over a 12-month period and comprises; face-to-face workshops, online learning and weekly accountability. Key milestones are set to ensure participants progress in their learning. The aim is to be able to manage the system in-house by the end of the programme."

The prospect has bought into you, your business and your solution, but doesn't exactly understand how it is going to work. This is not so much about the end result or what they have bought. It is more about what happens next. Confusion at this point doesn't help, and can cause the buyer to withdraw. Consider using graphics or brochures to describe the implementation process in detail. Not only will this help them understand, but it will convey a sense of professionalism.

Hard documents are out of fashion, but well written brochures and terms sheets can be invaluable. While your buyer may be attentive during the course of your meeting, much of what is actually discussed gets gradually forgotten, and what has registered may bear little relation to what you said. This is where a brochure is an excellent tool to summarise what you would like the prospect to take away. The content essentially lifts the answers from the *Positioning* section: Who are your target clients? What are their problems? How do you solve them? What's the result? And what's your credibility. After the meeting, when the prospect reviews potential suppliers, the documents you leave, will be a huge asset working in your favour.

At this stage, you should disclose your pricing structure. I can't stress enough, the importance of having a range of clearly defined costing alternatives. Talking about pricing can be uncomfortable for some people. If however, you have followed your process, explored the problems and presented a credible solution, then the prospect's investment is already being set against the cost of the problem. It's worth considering a pricing sheet, with exactly what's included, and what isn't. Don't rely on verbal pricing; this will again lead to misunderstanding as they try to recall what it included.

Decision time. It is now time, for the prospect to decide how to move forward. The most common response in a sales meeting is, *"Yes, we like what you're proposing but need to think about it."* This pleases the salesperson, who sees it as one step from a signature on the dotted line. But this answer can cover a multitude of underlying positions. From genuinely interested, and likely to sign, to interested but not right now, to no interest at all, just being polite.

Your challenge is to get clarity. Keep those who are interested in your pipeline and remove those who are not. This is difficult for salespeople as traditional sales tells you that an interested person is a lead, and leads are what you need to make a sale, and what your boss judges you on. Truth is, keeping people in your pipeline who are not genuine prospects is a mistake. They waste your time at the expense of finding real leads and they make your pipeline misleading. Finally, it denigrates the role of the salesperson. The job should be about having valuable conversations with your equal, not making them, and you, feel uncomfortable with endless chase-up emails and phone calls.

The way to weed out the genuine from the fake is, as before, with smart questioning. Don't fall into the trap of accepting the 'encouraging' response. You must challenge prospects, in a nurturing way, to find out if they are genuinely keen to progress, or question why, if they cannot. If it's a legitimate reason, then, agree the next step. This could be a call or meeting booked, to discuss specifics, such as; timescales, pricing, staffing or product compatibility. The purpose of which is to provide definitive answers and reassurance to their concerns. If they turn out to be a poor lead, then simply add them to your nurture campaign (newsletters, vlogs, blogs). Remove them from your pipeline, with a note to call them after a given period.

H. Handover

This is about getting the prospect's agreement on what happens next. At the close of the meeting, both sides should be clear about the next step. Are they interested and want to continue? Are they interested but can't continue at the moment? Or are they just not interested?

If they are keen to progress, you need to have the next steps mapped out i.e. client on-boarding, which covers XYZ, and agree dates for getting the senior management team together for a half-day session. Payment terms also need to be agreed. If there are any further issues, it's better to find out now rather than later.

While this is a good position to be in, and even though all the key terms have been covered, the sale can still collapse after this meeting. It's therefore important to test every assumption, while still face-to-face, as it's often hard to get your prospects on the phone again, let alone face-to-face!

MATCH summary

A standard sales system gives you and your team consistency and enables clear and effective management. We've addressed key aspects of the sales meeting and built a process that gives the best chance of moving the prospect forward. The MATCH method covers the 5-key areas to develop a dynamic sales system. This model will ensure the prospect is clear that you are a credible professional with an in-depth knowledge of their challenges. By understanding the main behavioural characteristics, you will be able to adapt your own style to match that of your prospect, so you don't alienate them before you have even begun!

You will also be able to qualify your prospects and know how to present your business solution in a clear and attractive way, closing or moving the sale forward. This process will give you greater confidence to manage your sales meetings, to ensure you don't lose the sale in the most common ways. By employing the MATCH method on a team-wide basis, you will be able to readily assess performance and see who is thriving or failing in each step, allowing you to resolve or reward performance.

PROGRESS

The final section in *Lead Conversion* is *Progress*. This refers to progressing the sale or opportunity. If the money's not in the bank, then the sale hasn't closed. If the buyer has said all the right things there is a temptation to rest on your laurels, but there are still risks at this stage. One is the client's post-sale experience does not map onto the pre-sale description. Clearly not the way to start a relationship and can lead to a very short-term engagement.

Another common failing is the follow-up. A recent study[2] found that only 1/3 of companies followed up after an enquiry. Sounds unbelievable, but my own experiences would suggest this figure could be even lower. It's particularly disappointing, given all the work that goes into finding and nurturing, that arguably the most important part of the sale is neglected.

Agreed follow-up. After all sales meetings, it's essential to follow-up. You have any number of choices available to you. You could send a letter with a summary of the meeting and the agreed next stage. Record the details of the meeting in your CRM and move the prospect to the appropriate stage in your pipeline. If you have not already done so, connect on LinkedIn.

Yes (Commitment). If you've won a new client, brief your delivery teams on what you have agreed and progress the prospect to your on-boarding process. Arrange a call or

---

[2] Conversica's 2015 Sales Effectiveness Report

meeting with the people who will be managing the account going forwards. Connect on LinkedIn

No, not now. For prospects that are a qualified 'not now', diarise the next activity and put them on a specific nurture campaign. Consider, if you can, making a referral or introduction to them. Record details on the CRM and move to the appropriate pipeline. Connect on LinkedIn

No, not ever. For 'not evers', record the meetings details on your CRM. Connect on LinkedIn. Much will depend on the reason for the 'no'. If they are clearly not right for you could they be for another firm? Are they a potential referral to one of your partners? Are they someone who could be a referral partner for you? If they have chosen one of your competitors, make sure you congratulate them (without sarcasm!). Try to ascertain why they made that decision and wish them well, keeping the door open should circumstances change.

Whatever path you choose for each, it should be documented and implemented consistently, with CRM integration.

The overriding principles of good selling

It's probably clear, that we are fans of constructive and ethical selling, the MATCH method reflects this. The following ethically sound principles should underpin all your business development activities.

Be inquisitive. As Stephen Covey preached, "Seek first to understand". This is a fundamental part of the MATCH process, in the problem identification and qualifying stages. Questioning is an important skill to allow you to understand your prospect's issues. Do they have a problem? How much does the problem matter to their business? Can they make the decision and can they afford it? Great questions distinguish you from the herd.

Listen. Listening is a vastly underrated and underused skill and most certainly in sales. It seems odd that we are taught to read and write at school, but not to listen. Active listening is much more than nodding politely. It means registering what the speaker is saying and acknowledging the points made. All too often we spend time formulating responses when someone else is talking. This means we rarely absorb what is being said.

Have integrity. It is only correct to try to win clients that need what you do. Winning the 'wrong' clients leads to business inefficiency and stores up future problems. To impress the 'right' type of clients, we should be entirely genuine and authentic. Accept you don't need the business of everyone you meet, or you can risk falling into the looking desperate category. Only pitch if there is a fit, to someone you can genuinely help.

Be professional. Never wing it. Be professional in every way, and follow a system for each stage of the buyer journey. There is sometimes resistance to following processes, with claims that it can stifle creativity, but a process is only the best way to do something at a particular time. Whether we like it or not, we always need to embrace inevitable change or get left behind. Treating sales as a profession should mean to always be developing your skills and knowledge.

Summary

People don't like to be sold to but they like to buy. Successful selling means getting people in a position where they want to buy rather than being pushed into something they may not want or need and regret later.

The three stages in *Lead Conversion* are designed to address the most important elements of selling, *Preparation*, *Execution* and *Progress*. Using systems and processes to manage sales activities converts unstructured, unprofessional selling into a science. Where consistent predicable results are available and new initiatives can be implemented and measured accurately.

Key takeaways

- ✓ Salespeople are made not born

- ✓ A sales system enables you to:

    - train your team on best practice

    - produce consistent results

    - remove reliance on individuals

    - manage your team effectively

    - quickly evaluate changes in tactics or strategy

- ✓ Build a system for each stage of the sale: Prepare, Execute and Progress

Step Four. ONGOING

"The purpose of business is to create and keep a customer."
Peter F. Drucker

In this section, we focus on how to deliver exceptional service to your clients. Essentially, what you deliver, how you deliver it and the related customer care. A sound customer experience provides high standards of delivery and service, and of course, a happy client.

To state the obvious, looking after your clients is important but there are two distinct elements to customer service which are often misunderstood. The first is the effectiveness of the solution or product i.e. does it actually work? The second is the client's experience during the engagement. This experience covers communication, support and feedback, i.e. did the supplier confirm the meeting, turn up on time, work with care and attention and to your satisfaction? All of this comes under customer service.

Ideally, businesses want to score well in both delivery and customer service, but it's not always the case. Most handle the delivery side reasonably well, but forget about the service aspect. Therefore, it's quite possible to have a situation where the job is done, but the client is not particularly happy.

Getting feedback from your customers is a fundamental part of achieving great customer satisfaction. This is culturally a difficult thing for businesses to do as there is a mistaken assumption that if the client doesn't contact you, then they are probably happy. Or when the feedback is negative it's taken personally or as a criticism. That's the wrong mindset. When used as part of your product and service development plan, feedback is invaluable. Encouraging clients to tell you what you can do better is a no-brainer!

Organisations that do focus on providing excellent customer satisfaction benefit from a team of loyal and happy clients, helping them to grow through positive word of mouth and active referrals. Setting up an effective account management process does require effort, but provides many efficiencies going forward. For example, an informative leaflet, email or brochure explaining how your product works or frequently asked questions, will shortcut the time-consuming process of dealing with constant client queries, and also please the customer. Your investment in producing the document makes better use of your time, and your client's, by dealing with potential enquiries before they are asked.

To achieve consistent delivery, it's essential to have a standard approach. Without it, it's impossible to know what is and isn't working. You have already mapped out your basic process delivery solution or method, in *Positioning*, now it's time to put that into a 'delivery framework'. Produce implementation guides, covering each element and include timing and accountability. Providing as much detail as possible here, will enable you to manage the process and produce consistency. It must be used as a template for all team members, including new recruits, to understand and 'pick up' the process easily. It can also be used in client on-boarding, to demonstrate how the engagement works, and the roles and responsibilities at each stage.

How you provide a good customer experience

Effective account management goes to the heart of your business. It enables consistent and high-level delivery, which in turn will contribute positively to customer satisfaction. Variability of delivery is not good but is incredibly common. Be it, a garage, or a legal practice, each person within that company will probably have a slightly different way of approaching the same task. In some cases, it will be a marginal difference; in others it will be significant. The challenge is to decide which is the best method. Once you've established this, you simply replicate it!

In the *Interest* section, we looked at building various sales activities using the three stage MAP method. The same approach is required for your delivery method. Managing a sales team who follow a system makes life much easier for both the supplier and the customer, in the same way as does having a delivery team who also follow a clearly defined and documented process.

MODEL: The steps in your delivery process (i.e. your 5-step process).

ARTICULATE: The processes for each step of the system, with key components of the delivery clearly defined. It requires skill to write in summary form as there are so many variables it's difficult to address them all. So, rather than seeking to mitigate every difference, look at the key parts of the delivery and summarise.

PERFORMANCE: Identify the KPIs that quickly and efficiently assess performance. For example, if a project has a two-week turn around, then a KPI may be on-time completion.

With the process defined, you now focus on training your team on delivery. A by-product of this simple approach is that it has a big impact on performance management as it enables you to track performance in the same way it does for sales. Rather than being a largely opaque area, you will have complete visibility about the delivery team's performance. This has huge benefits to your management, training, development and recruitment processes.

It also allows for continuous improvement. Enhancing delivery, without a process is very difficult. It's like doing a crossword in the dark. It's impossible without knowing the starting point. This is further compounded with a team who all have a slightly different approach.

Note: Make sure you don't produce a passive manual gathering dust on a shelf. It must be a workable and practical set of processes that anyone can pick up and use.

"Your most unhappy customers are your greatest source of learning."
Bill Gates

Two of the most common frustrations in running a business are sales and people related. A big contributor to management issues are unclear roles and responsibilities. For example, a website designer might spend two weeks working on drafts for one client, and only two days for another. Left to his own devices accountability is unclear. Are they ahead or behind, on a project and where should they be? A visible delivery process means the client will know how you work and will have bought into it.

McDonalds was a forerunner of the process-driven model. Ultimately creating a multibillion-dollar empire. It was started by two brothers and was likely to remain a modest operation until Ray Croc had an idea to replicate the model across America. You may not like McDonalds, as a culinary experience, but they basically wrote the book when it comes to delivering consistency. Indeed, its success owes much to this decision. As a result, wherever you are in the world your Big Mac will taste exactly the same. Impressive, given all the variables that go into making it. Ambitious and successful organisations build effective systems and processes that are scalable, deliver a high customer satisfaction rating and reduce reliance on key people.

With systems, processes and KPIs assigned, you can have meaningful management conversations about delivery. What is working well and what is not? Where are you in the process for each client? Who is performing well and who isn't? The results will give you the basis for change, improvement, and crucially, you'll see their impact.

Are you Aldi or Armani? Customer service excellence is a choice not an accident. When deciding how you want your customers to think of you, you must first decide who you are and where you want to pitch your service. There's often some confusion surrounding this, as not all businesses aspire to be a 'Rolls Royce'. A Novotel can provide excellent customer service in the same way the Ritz can as Novotel customers will be judging their experience related to the price paid, and not benchmarking it against the Ritz.

You can't aim to be the best if your business model does not allow it. As Frei & Morriss explain in the book "Uncommon Service", by being good at something, you must also be bad at something. You can choose to be no-frills, or be completely focused on providing outstanding service. Some businesses, like low-cost airlines, have models with basic customer service. For them to be low-cost they can't be high-service, the economics don't work. In the same way online organisations build systems to automate the customer's journey that seamlessly guide them through to a transaction. This model cuts out the human element and customers are happy, as long as it works.

The benefits of a clearly defined target market are again important. It's hard to please a variety of customer groups who all want and expect different things. As much as we would like to provide an outstanding service for everyone, it's just not possible to achieve. How well would Ryanair do, if it started to target luxury travellers with its current model? Possibly one battle even Michael O'Leary wouldn't win.

Whatever model you choose, it must work financially. The only common goal is that the customer is happy, or even better, delighted with the experience! So what can you afford to do to provide an excellent customer experience and still make money?

Many business owners love to tell you how well they look after their customers and how much their customers love them. You see mission statements claiming to put customers at the heart of everything they do. How often is this just 'marketing-speak' with no evidence to support it. Businesses that have a coordinated approach to customer service will have invested in a process to request, use, and digest feedback. If you are new to the whole idea of structured account management, it may well seem daunting but it is a vital job.

The customer service plan (how your clients experience your delivery) is overlaid onto the delivery process. There are loads of great individual customer services ideas out there, but rather than cobble a few together, a coordinated plan is needed which covers all the key parts involved in making an excellent customer experience. The main elements are:

- Communication
- Support
- Feedback
- Delight

Communication

Customers are more patient than you think and will forgive almost anything, *if* you communicate with them regularly.

Regular communication makes clients feel valued and cared for. The absence of this creates an environment where they feel little in the way of loyalty and are therefore open to the charms of your competitors. To keep happy long-term customers, the bare minimum is a consistent channel of regular communication.

For a specific engagement or project, it's a good idea to ensure that your clients know exactly what is going to happen during the work and when updates or feedback will be given. Excellent communication need not necessarily create more work. You can create email templates or guides to answer many of the questions that typically arise.

"The successful man is the one who finds out what is the matter with his business before his competitors do."
Roy L. Smith

Support

Great companies support their clients not only on how to use their product, but also with related information, such as product upgrades, new applications or relevant industry developments. It's desirable that your clients are using your product or service to its full potential to gain maximum benefit. Businesses that take clients money and then don't worry if they never use the product should be concerned. It's an unsustainable and unethical practice.

Hands-up if you've ever done the post-Christmas Health Club guided tour? Feeling inspired, after a period of overindulgence, you must join. Unfortunately you do. Then, the sofa and TV beckons. A year later, after a handful of visits, you find you've joined the most expensive gym in the world!

You can argue that it's just the health club model. Yet, I would say they should strive to engage with members, especially new ones, to get traction. They could be creating lifetime members who make fitness and well-being an integral part of their lives. Plus, the revenue from that model would far outweigh the 12-month random attendance approach. As well as being bad business, it's simply wrong to take money for a service which is not used.

"We believe that customer service shouldn't be just a department; it should be the entire company."
Tony Hsieh

Whatever your business, you need to consider client use. Are they optimising the product or service to get maximum benefit for their outlay? And are they enjoying it? Much of this can be addressed at the delivery stage. You can create a journey designed to get clients fully on board and using the product optimally. Then, using monitoring and further training, you can further strengthen the role and use of the product in the client's business.

Building a client community, either online or face-to-face, facilitates the sharing of ideas and experiences on how best to use your product to support their business. It's all about adding value which will also benefit you. This can increase use of the product or service, provide insights and ideas for future products, create marketing-friendly third-party endorsements, save you time and create a community feel.

> Lush is a quirky ethical cosmetics company that has grown to over 1000 shops worldwide. In addition to providing a unique product, the company has focused on providing a remarkable and innovative customer experience. They regularly rank in the top 10 of customer service ratings. Needless to say, staff training is a key part of this. The shop design is based on customers engaging and touching the products, making the shop look part greengrocer part cosmetics. There are also in-store demonstrations which give clients the opportunity to try before they buy. A recent development has been faster mobile based tills which mean staff, can help customers quicker. Their approach, highlights how far behind many other retailers are. Sales and post-sale support is a fundamental part of any business. If done well it may lead to a sale. If done amazingly well, it may lead to a lifelong customer

Whatever information you do share to support your clients, must be of value to them. While the Internet is a rich source of data, the challenge is being able to find relevant information that your clients will find useful. Fortunately, when you look away from the mainstream news sites, there are many smaller specialist news feeds producing interesting content. You will need to do some research to find the best ones in your industry. By sharing relevant content, your clients will see you as a supporter and valued partner, rather than just another supplier. Do consider the use of newsletters carefully as most don't add much value, are not widely read and can detract from the relationship. It may be more worthwhile sending occasional emails, and then only when you have something useful to say.

Feedback

To harness the power of your customers' experiences, improve your product and strengthen the bond with your clients, you need to build a framework that is regularly seeking, and using, feedback. This involves three principal elements:

Ask: So many organisations claim their clients are really happy. But, as they never ask them, it's neither valid nor objective. A structured customer feedback system will enable you to objectively measure your client's views on your product or service by regularly canvassing them.

Fix: When a problem is flagged up, you need to fix it. Take the feedback graciously and review it objectively. Not all client complaints are 100% legitimate, but you should approach them all as if they are. Once you understand the underlying issue, it should be addressed so the situation or problem doesn't recur. It's also vital that you go further than the minimum action required to put right the issue to the customer's satisfaction. Be grateful to them for their feedback. This simple strategy converts potential detractors to supporters at no cost!

Measure: How good is your customer service? The only accurate way to know is by measurement. Then improve it by first benchmarking then setting a target for your initiatives, to see what effect they are having.

For feedback to be valid there needs to be an ongoing timetable of requests during the engagement, or over a defined period. You can map a programme of feedback onto the delivery timetable. For example, ask for general feedback, say, every six months, and then delivery feedback after each piece of work is concluded.

Another benefit in having an ongoing feedback process is that you can act on the information before it is too late. Often, problems or issues are uncovered at the end of an engagement. At this late stage there can be a build-up of frustration and additional work to correct the issue. By gaining feedback early, you can resolve issues before they escalate. It is important to remember, that as well as the feedback you proactively ask for, clients may voluntarily give you their own views which, as with all feedback, should be used and acted upon.

Build your customer feedback programme using the MAP method. Consider at what points feedback will be requested, over a given timeframe. Decide how to ask for feedback, Face-to-face, online, or over the phone. KPIs include the number of attempts to get feedback (not everyone will complete), number of responses and, most fundamentally, the actual feedback scores! Remember, you can't dip your toe in the water, as 'bits' of feedback offer little in the way of insight. So if you are measuring performance build the framework and then ensure you are using it regularly.

Closing the loop. When you do get feedback from clients, negative or positive, it is essential that the information is acted on. Closing the loop means you first address the issue to the client's satisfaction. Next, fix the problem that caused the issue. Finally, record the problem and explore if there needs to be a more in-depth fix to ensure no other clients experience the same problem.

An example from a recent visit to a local restaurant illustrates what not closing the loop looks like. During the meal one of our group complained to the waitress that there was far too much seasoning in their food, making it inedible. The waitress apologised profusely and said she would tell the chef. So far, so good. However, that was the last we heard on the matter.

This is not untypical of what many of us experience day to day in our personal or working lives. The simple close the loop approach, ensures positive outcomes. The correct way to handle the issue would have been:

1. **Resolve the problem**. "Sorry this was not up to standard. Can we get you an alternative dish as a way of making amends? And, of course, we'll remove it from the bill".

2. **Find out what went wrong**. Was it a one-off chef error, or a poor recipe?

3. **Use the information**. If the recipe was good but a new chef couldn't get it right, then retraining would be needed. If it was poor, remove it and add recipe tasting to your menu planning.

In our case, we received none of this and as a result, left the restaurant unimpressed. The business unnecessarily exposed themselves to negative reviews, poor word of mouth and as a group of fourteen, a not insignificant loss of repeat customers. Frustratingly, by just closing the loop they could have easily turned potential detractors into supporters.

Some may view this as over compensating, as the customer is not always right. True, sometimes they are wrong, but it's rarer that you think. Most people are not trying to be difficult or have a free meal. There will always be one or two naturally awkward customers, willing to try it on, but on balance it's worth responding to all complaints in the same way. Damaging PR, from those exposing badly resolved complaints, never looks good – especially when so much negative customer service is shared on social media.

Delight

The whole subject of customer service is misunderstood by so many organisations. The most common response to the question. Are you good at customer service? Is, *"Yes our clients love us!"*. Many cite the fact they get few complaints, or have low customer turnover. Occasionally this may be true, but it's not an accurate interpretation, nor does it provide a benchmark. Besides, does it really mean your customers are happy? You only need to look at the banking industry, where there is low client turnover, but also low customer satisfaction, to see that long term doesn't necessarily equal happy clients.

A research report conducted by Bain & Company and Satmetrix, found that 80% of 360 firms surveyed believed they delivered a "superior experience" to their clients. But astonishingly only 8% of those firms' clients believed these brands were really delivering. An illustration of how wrongly some companies perceive themselves!

The only way to really know how happy your customers are, is by measurement. When it comes to obtaining a good understanding of your clients' relative satisfaction it's not that easy. Many organisations make the effort to develop a customer satisfaction programme, but critically fail to add measurement to their process. This is unfortunate, as they are putting the effort in, but missing the most important element.

There are several ways to measure customer satisfaction. One of the most popular is the Net Promoter Score (NPS). Created by Bain & Company, the NPS is based on a single question which they discovered most correlated to customer loyalty, which is:

"What is the likelihood that you would recommend company X to a friend or colleague?"

The NPS measures the willingness of customers to recommend a company's products or services to others. It is used to measure the customer's overall satisfaction and loyalty to a company's product or service. They are asked to give a score between 0 to 10 and based on their rating, customers are then classified into three categories: detractors, passives and promoters. A simple calculation gives you an all important number, the key to managing and improving. See www.netpromoter.com for more information.

The Net Promoter Score, is not a solution to your whole customer satisfaction process, but it does address the central issue of measurement. It can also be an indicator of growth, i.e. high NPS scores are typical of high-growth companies. So, by building a strategy to increase your NPS score, you may also be building a higher growth business. The system means you can quickly work out the proportion of happy, neutral and unhappy customers you have. However, it's not designed to give an in-depth insight into individual customer issues.

> Founded in 1999, Zappos.com is an online shoe and apparel shop. It was bought by Amazon in 2009 but still operates as separate business at arm's length. It was started when the founder saw a gap in the market i.e. buying a wide selection of shoes online. It is feted for its customer service and quality, offering a wide choice, free shipping and returns. To make this happen it places the highest importance on its staff, given that they are the ones who can make the strategy work. The company is completely focused on ecommerce with excellent customer service. It has embraced social media, has guides, product information and lots of other relevant content. It is famous for the quality of its call centre staff. They are expertly trained and, amazingly, have no time limit on how long it takes to solve a customer query – apparently some calls have lasted hours! In terms of its customer care strategy, it has broken the mould. Buying shoes online, something that you would not expect to work, but is now a huge business. Much of this is down to the customer experience. Buyers know that they will be well looked after, and are pleased that if they don't want their shoes, for whatever reason, they can return them simply and easily. By being outstanding they have built a valuable enterprise that just happens to focus on shoes.

The NPS system itself has its critics and advocates. I'm of the opinion that while it may not be perfect, it has many things going for it. First, it tells you, relatively accurately, what your customers think about you. It does not tell you how to fix the problem, but using the question strategically you can work out the cause. Second, it's simple, easy to use and intuitive and as a result should have higher than average completion rates.

What is important to your client? We have seen that people buy for their own reasons and not because of your features and benefits. It may be based on price, after-sales support or because they liked the salesperson. Everyone values things differently. It's important to understand, what your customer cares about, as this affects the ongoing delivery. To make your delivery as successful as possible try to establish what the client values or cares most about so you can focus on those areas.

Summary

The aim with an account management plan is to create customers who are long-term loyal fans, who can help you grow your business by actively referring business. The prime focus of any company should be its existing customers; the challenge is to meet both the needs of existing and new clients.

To create a consistently high-level of customer satisfaction, a framework is required which incorporates all the important customer care elements to ensure consistently high service. This starts with an understanding of the problem you are solving (established in *Positioning*) to ensure your product delivers. Then defining your delivery process with the required detail to solve each set of challenges at every stage of the engagement. Use KPIs to manage the implementation and ensure consistent delivery. Finally, it's important to be constantly striving for improvement. This attitude is vital for this model to work.

With the product delivery side addressed, attention turns to the customer experience. While it's true all airlines will transport you across the globe, not all will send a limousine to collect you, and drop you off at the other end. The first stage in creating a remarkable customer journey is recognising where you rank, and where your business model allows. Are you, no-frills, luxury, or somewhere between? By knowing this, you can design your customer journey to reflect this through all contact points.

The building blocks of a customer service programme are: communication, ongoing support to optimise product use, canvassing customer opinion, and closing the loop with any client issues in a way that delights your customer and improves your delivery.

The collection and dissemination of client feedback is often neglected. In reality, it's a fundamental part of a good customer service programme and ongoing product development. Rather than fearing feedback, both positive and negative responses should be embraced. Use it to improve your offering for the benefit of new and existing clients – and ultimately your business!

Key takeaways

- ✓ Current clients should be your business's #1 priority

- ✓ Decide where to pitch your service: no-frills or luxury

- ✓ MAP your account management process

- ✓ Embrace client feedback

- ✓ Measure your customer satisfaction and set targets for improvement

- ✓ Make customer care a strategic business goal

Step Five. TRACK

Anyone who's attempted to tackle a new initiative, be it business or personal, will know that actually putting it into practice can be daunting, and is rarely straightforward. A brilliant course, a series of inspirational podcasts, an excellent self-help book, can all clearly illustrate the value in making changes, and yet, one still fails to act on the advice given.

The final piece in the PILOT method is to ensure the framework, systems and processes are implemented, measured, managed and improved in line with the plan. The initial part of this module completes any outstanding elements of the infrastructure, processes and collateral. Next is a programme of training covering all the new methods. Then it's the process to manage each of the sales activities and people. Finally creating a culture of continuous improvement

Activity is the hallmark of all successful businesses. The classic salesman is a dynamo, pitching to anyone and everyone. And yes, this method does work but it's flawed. As discussed, it can be highly ineffective and difficult, if not impossible, to manage. The *Positioning* step alone makes your activities much more effective and efficient, as it ensures you focus your efforts on valuable customers who are aligned with your product. Yet the single most important requirement is always the selling activity itself.

Whatever you do, make sure that your team is not spending undue amounts of time building systems and processes. Progress beats perfection, every time. So get them built and start using them ASAP.

Inventory

In following the PILOT process, you will have created and developed a wide range of materials many individual business systems, sales and marketing materials, and checklists. With so many, it's important to make an *Inventory* of all your business development processes and collateral. To enable team collaboration

look at software such as Google Drive or Dropbox. Google Docs also has a simple flowchart creation programme called Drawio where you can produce your MAP process flowcharts.

All of this can appear a little intimidating. However, it's a one-off job which, when completed, will be used (and adapted) over many years to come. It's what is needed to get your team working to a consistent practice. If you miss one piece of collateral, for example an email template, you will quickly discover the gaps in the process when you come to do that activity. So it's important to get this right now, to avoid delay, later.

Your business development processes will principally be created around, *Prospecting* (finding customers), *Lead Conversion* (winning customers) and *Account Management* (keeping and growing customers). The inventory for each starts with a MAP diagram. This covers your; outline structure, required collateral, and KPIs. Below is a reminder of the MAP structure.

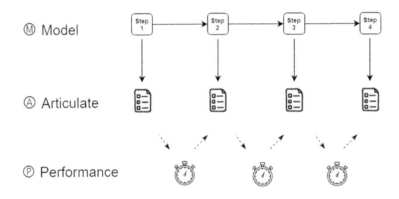

The *Model* element is self-explanatory – it's the steps in the system. The *Articulate* stage (how it's done) is where you will be creating collateral such as templates, emails, scripts, agendas and brochures. It's important that a filing system is created and is easily accessible, as the whole team will be using it. The *Performance* part will have identified KPIs to be used in the *KPI Tracker*. It's also a good idea to keep a master list of KPIs, by activity, so you can easily refer to those used previously, as you might need them again.

An inventory checklist can be created using a simple spreadsheet *(see below)*, showing the three elements of the

MAP method across the top and the activities down the left hand-side. In each activity box add the person's name responsible for production and colour code each for status e.g. red if outstanding, green if complete, orange if in progress.

Activity	Model	Articulate	Performance
Networking (Paul)	✓	✗	✓
Inbound (Sarah)	✓	✗	✗
Referrals (John)	✓	✗	✓

Implementation

> *"Knowledge is not power. Implementation is power."*
> Garrison Wynne

With the infrastructure *Inventory* complete, it's time to embed the systems and processes throughout the organisation. This is always a sensitive area, as people don't like change and can see the new approach as a threat to them and their position and so it requires careful handling.

In some companies, staff have created mini-fiefdoms which make it hard to manage and introduce new ideas. While this is understandable, the overriding priority must be the long-term health of the business and its ability to succeed, which in turn will support the workforce going forwards. Unfortunately, a common approach to implementing change is done by the well-intentioned, but misguided, email laying out new sales targets, or new strategies. This is poor management and makes it difficult to get traction with the staff, who typically ignore, push back or worse; sabotage the plans.

Organisational cultures in more enlightened businesses are a very different beast to older more traditional ones. They have cultivated an environment that not only makes them an attractive place to work, but has recognised the need, across the organisation, to be commercial. Another positive characteristic is the desire to create a collegiate feel where each member of staff has bought into the purpose of the business, as well as their individual role.

The idea of a happy workforce increasing productivity is now gaining acceptance. So it makes sense to develop job satisfaction and instil a feeling staff are contributing to a wider cause and doing something of real value. There are still too many businesses where employees are just doing a job and clearly have little enthusiasm for their role or the company. Imagine what message this sends to the outside world, suppliers, clients and potential customers? If you value your staff, then the process of redefining your business development activities should involve them.

While the PILOT method is heavily process-based, your people still need to learn and master the methods identified. You will have invested a significant amount of time putting it all together. If you have been open and involved them, your staff will know about the business development initiatives and are much more likely to buy into them. If not, you will need to run training sessions so they can see what's involved, their roles and the likely implications.

To make an inventory of all the training required refer initially to the system maps you created earlier. Specific training will vary from role to role, but a starting point is to communicate to staff the rationale behind the aims and changes to business practices. The *Positioning* section dealt with the ability of all staff being able to describe the company in a consistent manner using the pitch. Another whole workforce activity is the use of social media to grow networks and support referral or partner opportunities.

Activity	Model	Articulate	Performance	Training
Networking	✓	✗	✓	✗
Inbound	✓	✗	✗	✗
Referrals	✓	✗	✓	✓

Training is fundamental to the success of your plans. Limited, or poor training, won't enable the systems and processes to work and you will be no further forward. A training plan needs to be created and implemented to embed the new methods. The MATCH sales system will need to be tailored to your business, with intensive initial training sessions followed by ongoing training programmes.

Evaluate

With the initial training complete and the processes set out, it's time to look at how you manage the various business development activities. The PILOT method enables simple and effective management by using metrics. It's important to review them to ensure you have selected the right ones. So how does this happen in the bedding down period, and then how is it managed day-to-day?

Managing and measuring performance is a fundamental part of running a business. The principle is the same as measuring performance in any activity. To improve your standard of golf, the first step is to know where you are at now, i.e. a 25 handicap. If you take lessons and practise five hours per week you can assess performance by comparing your new handicap against the one at the start. This seems obvious, but so many businesses begin their business improvement initiatives without a clear way to assess them, e.g. *"Next year we would like to be better at customer care"*. Better than what? It's therefore essential to know where you are today or your starting values.

> *"If you can't measure it, you can't improve it."*
> Peter Drucker

Another critical benefit in measurement, is to support management. If you have a set of activities against which you are assessed, then it's hard to explain to your boss that you haven't done any of them. The old adage is remarkably accurate; *"What gets measured gets done!"*

Deciding what you measure is key to being able to manage and grow. To some, KPIs are overkill and complicate what is, often seen as, a straightforward task. I accept, there is probably some truth in this. If you have too many the process becomes unwieldy and momentum is lost. So while we talk a lot about KPIs, a few valuable numbers are much more important than too many.

We looked earlier at the inefficient approach to sales displayed by many salespeople – spending too much time on noncore jobs instead of selling. To give them focus, and stop them engaging in peripheral activities, you can set KPIs solely related to new business acquisition.

In addition, sales management should be based on activities, within their control, e.g. leading indicators such as networking, prospecting, writing blogs and asking for referrals. You can't control the actual sale no matter how much pressure you give the sales team.

Every business will have their own unique set of KPIs, as business development activities vary from business to business. You have already defined your key processes, now it's a question of extracting the few metrics that are fundamental in the implementation and performance tracking. A few standard numbers for all businesses include; lead indicators, conversion rates and results (sales).

Manage

Management of salespeople is notoriously problematic. Alec Baldwin, gives a good example in the film *Glengarry Glen Ross,* screaming "A.B.C. always-be-closing", at his hapless team. This attitude seems to have permeated into sales teams everywhere. Unfortunately, it doesn't work. No matter how much you shout, or try to stimulate performance through bravado, it won't change the facts. Without training, a sales system, a target market, a USP and KPIs, you are making life very hard and all the motivational speeches in the world won't make any difference.

It doesn't need to be that way. The PILOT method makes management a visible process. The ability to hold salespeople accountable is one of the most important benefits it brings. Rather than trying to work out what's in or out of the pipeline, or how busy an individual salesperson has been over the month, the numbers will tell you precisely.

> *"The true measure of the value of any business leader and manager is performance."*
> Brian Tracy

With your systems, processes, collateral, and KPIs prepared, it's time to consider activity targets. This needs to be done in two stages. First, you have to collect data to give your opening or benchmark rates. Then, set initial targets which are not too high and not too low. If they are too low you'll get hit with lower sales. Equally, if they are set too high, people won't buy into the process and will lose interest. Set a time frame which allows you to collect a significant and meaningful amount of data to make your initial numbers accurate.

Next, assess the information. You will begin to see the relationship between the activities and conversion rates, and be able to adjust your targets with more accuracy. This is a fundamental benefit in employing a system. Look at your resources and your conversion rates then set targets that are in line with your growth plans. This will give you the powerful element of predictability. When you know your metrics, you can turn on and off the sales tap depending on your aspirations.

Accountability

With systems in place, the management of your business development activities should look considerably different.

Instead of ambiguous conversations discussing the likelihood of a particular client converting, you will be focusing on clear progress in relation to stated activity targets. As you have built up your processes you will have determined who in your organisation will be able to perform each task.

Individual sales activities cover a wide range of jobs from new business meetings to building LinkedIn contacts. Use spreadsheets to monitor and measure activity with responsibility assigned. Coordination at weekly meetings will focus largely on the performance against the targets. You should aim to meet weekly and have a live *KPI Tracker* spreadsheet (below). This gives real-time performance against targets. The weekly meetings will enable feedback and further analysis, with coaching sessions to address any areas of underperformance.

As you can see below, there can be great simplicity in accountability by using numbers. You can, if you so wish, measure an employee's performance with a single blended number. In this example the composite weekly number - John's performance at week three was at 70%.

Staff member: John	Target	Week 1	Week 2	Week 3
Past client engagement	10	9	11	6
Blogs written	1	1	1	2
Referrals asked for	5	6	8	3
Performance		100%	125%	70%

Sales meeting

You can already hear the collective groans from the staff at the mere mention of another meeting. Most people have a negative view of meetings as in their experience they are unstructured, last way too long and achieve little. However, you can't manage without them, so it's important they're done properly.

The first thing to establish is the purpose of the meeting. If it is a sales meeting to review prospecting, sales and KPIs, then that's what it should be about. Where meetings get bogged down is when they start to cross over into other associated areas. It is important to keep the focus with any related issues addressed separately, otherwise the meeting is open to hijack. A clear agenda is the backbone of the meeting. A chairperson may sound rather grandiose but they are invaluable in keeping all on track and focused.

You should aim to have weekly sales meetings, and a longer, possibly full team meeting on a monthly basis as a minimum. It is best to organise a regular day and time to meet. This creates consistency, sets expectations, and individual coaching and accountability sessions can be arranged around it.

For the more in-depth monthly meetings, you can include improvements to your activities, through skills development, changes in technology or feedback from clients. Also consider including: training exercises, market updates, competition and performance in relation to strategic business goals.

163

Taking notes helps with accountability. There is a skill involved in meeting notes, as you don't want a transcript of the meeting, but you still need to summarise the key points and actions (and identify who is taking them). By keeping them short and punchy they are much more likely to be read by others, and the required action taken.

Make sure the meeting always starts and finishes on time. Deal with constant latecomers separately, but don't delay for them. Ensure all participants are well prepared. If they need numbers, correspondence or other collateral, they must have them.

Example: weekly sales meeting agenda

1. **Sales update.** What sales have been closed, the value and next steps in delivery (handover to delivery team)? Review sales lost and lessons learned.

2. **Prospecting update.** Look at the activity vs. targets for each salesperson and related conversion rates, leads created and value.

3. **Pipeline update.** What's in the pipeline? It's vital there is a focus on a universal language related to your sales system. This may be the client's that are "Stage 2" qualified, i.e. they've tested the product and have the ability to make the buying decision. This makes the pipeline realistic and clear. Avoid comments like, *"they really love it and will definitely be doing something"*.

4. **Key actions** required before next meeting. Clearly defined, with person responsible and a due date.

5. **Lessons**: There will be always something disclosed that can have an impact on a process or a sales skill that should be noted and shared. Having a learning section provides the opportunity for improvement.

6. **Make it fun**: People work better when they are in a positive relaxed mindset, as they are more willing to contribute and open up about challenges or problems.

The overriding rules of the meeting are to keep them short and focused on the key metrics and required actions. This will ensure minimum time spent for maximum productivity. If you find your meetings ramble on for hours, you're doing something wrong.

People Management

As we've seen, the softer people skills are not necessarily abundant in the world of sales management, and too often salespeople are promoted on the (mistaken basis) that if they are good at sales, ergo they must be good at sales management. If the salesperson is not trained or prepared for the specific role of management, they will fail in the new role. This creates the double whammy of losing an effective salesperson and gaining an ineffective manager.

Good management is about getting the best out of your team. Some of the key elements in achieving this are:

- Coaching– to develop the individual's performance (see below)
- Ongoing training – to improve skills and learn new ones
- Recruitment / resource management – finding talent and cutting non-performers

- Monitoring – sales activity by team and individual against targets
- Revenue and profitability – against the business goals
- Strategic input – on the sales process and targets

Improve

With any new significant business initiative there are typically two distinct phases. First, get the new systems and staff behaviours embedded so the managers can run it. Second, to constantly be finding new ways to improve.

> *"Amateurs practice till they get it right; professionals practice till they can't get it wrong".*
> George W Loomis

All great organisations, large or small, seek to improve. A dynamic organisation that's constantly striving to do its best is a more interesting and exciting place to work, which can only be positive for the business, owners, staff and customers.

Too many companies view staff training as a cost rather than an investment, which results in a reluctance to spend money on what is seen as luxury. It is understandable to some extent, especially if they have engaged in training in the past which did not have a positive impact, or was poor.

Training is not designed to be just a 'nice thing to do', or a one-off, but should form a standard part of every person's employment. Professional sports people do endless training, much more than actually playing. The same is true for amateurs, who also spend significant amounts of time honing their skills. It's time to view your staff as professionals. They are paid to do their job to the best of their abilities, so what are you doing to develop and improve them?

Training can come in a wide range of formats. Some are on a specific subject; others are just general feel-good sessions. While generally, training is a good idea, be careful not to undertake any old course just to tick the training box. A well thought out programme will comprise a mixture of activities, but should have an overriding aim of improvement.

Business owners have a choice to develop and improve their staff. It's a shame that some can't see the relationship between developing staff and the performance of their business. At the end of the day, a business is only as strong as its people and investment in your people, not only helps you grow, it wins their loyalty and support.

> *"Train people well enough so they can leave,*
> *treat them well enough so they don't want to."*
> Richard Branson

Some organisations that do buy into the positives that training brings, struggle with the fear that their well-trained people will leave. Yes, this is a risk, but it's overstated, and the alternative of not training them, is much less attractive.

Coaching

Your people are your greatest asset. How you lead, motivate and inspire, has a huge impact on the success of your venture. One of the essential ways to help your people grow and flourish is through coaching. The terms 'coaching' and 'business coach' have proliferated in the business support market over recent years. As with many ideas, the original purpose has been lost. It seems that now, anyone who advises businesses is labelled as a coach, but this is wrong. It may seem a trivial difference, but coaching is a very specific and valuable activity. The seminal business book by Timothy Gallwey, *The Inner Game of Tennis* describes coaching as, unlocking a person's potential to maximise their own performance, in essence helping them to learn, rather than teaching them.

There are innumerable benefits to coaching your employees. The most dynamic and forward-thinking businesses don't talk about managing their staff, but rather coaching them. This principle is completely logical. All employees have different strengths and weaknesses. Training fails in this area as it assumes everyone is at the same level, whereas coaching is about focusing on an individual's specific abilities.

The role of a coach is not something many managers will be familiar with or, if they are, they make the mistake of assuming coaching and training are the same thing. The relationship between manager and team member is also different. It's more of a level playing field with the coaching taking place between equals.

The coaching process is based on the manager and employee initially focusing on the skills gap between where they are now and where they need to be. A common starting point is benchmarking strengths and weaknesses, which is much easier for a team following a system. The coach facilitates the development of the employee through questioning and discussion. This results in the employee discovering the path forward themselves, which is much more powerful than the default method of being told.

"The biggest room in the world is the room for improvement."
Helmut Schmidt

There are many reasons to make coaching a part of your management practices. It can increase the staff bond and loyalty as employees value personal development. It has a positive impact on performance, which in turn, benefits the organisation. Continuous improvement leads to a culture of learning and development, making the workforce much more valuable. And in terms of investment, coaching is relatively cost-effective as it is largely done in-house by existing staff.

GE is a great example of a company that understands the importance of employee development. In 1956, they built the Crotonville management centre, essentially a GE University. GE spends hundreds of millions of dollars each year on staff training. Jack Welsh, the former CEO, was largely responsible for transforming the company into one of the world's largest companies. One of his primary beliefs was his role in growing others. This involved training and challenging his teams. This approach to training was not done because it was a nice thing to do for his staff, it was essential for the competitiveness of his business.

In today's business world, there are many gadgets, programs and apps designed to make life easier, from coordinating online meeting booking to automated email responders. However, one essential tool is a CRM, which is basically a client database. In the past CRM systems have been 'clunky' sometimes creating more work than value. Over recent years they have become indispensable as improved functionality allows you to do all manner of clever things, such as building visual sales pipelines to move clients along as they complete stages in the sales process. They are also invaluable in your account management work, telling you when a particular activity related to a specific client is due. The latest systems now crossover into inbound lead generation. Some can capture leads from your website directly, that are then entered into a relevant email nurture series.

At a basic level CRM systems ensure complete visibility of your business, so managers and team members can see the full account history. This mitigates the risk of duplication, and also enables all staff to be fully briefed about the client before each contact point.

Summary

The prevailing business and political environment, if you believe the newspapers, is set to create a difficult time for the economy, which can be distracting. However, the truth is it's largely what we do in our own business that is of much more significance. Before you worry about external events, over which you have no control, look at your own venture to ensure you are doing everything you can to optimise your performance.

The most important part of any initiative is the implementation. So often, great ideas stop before this stage, as day-to-day issues get in the way. Or, if it is done, it's done poorly. The PILOT method is clear and practical, but wide-reaching, and will require time and effort to implement. Once in place you will have created a framework for your business development programme. Namely the processes, the collateral and the KPIs. The initial implementation period will essentially be testing and bedding-in your model to obtain your benchmark measurements. These relate to the most important metrics. This phase will continue until you have built up enough data. The timeframe is related to your sales cycle. If your product is high-value or has a long-sale cycle it will take longer to collect the numbers.

Once you have your data it is time to train and coach your teams to ensure they are constantly performing and improving. You can look at specific initiatives in each process to effect change, with the knowledge that you will have good visibility of the results.

Lucozade is one of the market leaders for energy drinks with over 50% of the market share. Since energy drinks are a relatively new phenomena and Lucozade has been going since the 1920's what changed? Believe it or not, Lucozade was originally pitched as a drink to help poorly children. The advertising reflected this, with images showing sick kids nursing a glass of the bright orange drink. However, as time went on, the role of the drink in convalescence became less attractive, and sales slumped. A significant reposition took place in the 1980's. A new tagline and endorsement, from super star Olympian, Daley Thompson set the company on the road to success. Since then it has gone from strength to strength, dominating the energy drink sector. It's ability to review, its product and client base, was fundamental in reworking its position and strategy. Without this approach to change, it's hard to see how the company would have survived.

The accountability section is simple and straightforward, KPIs are assigned to team members who will be assessed against them. This applies to frontline sales and the wider organisation. They are more obvious for the sales team, but to develop as a commercial organisation where everyone has a part to play, then the other roles must also be clear and have accountability. Their involvement may be as little as just knowing the company pitch.

By developing a culture of continuous improvement, you should see many more staff-generated initiatives to strengthen and improve the way you work. Using targets will make the idea of refining more intuitive and easier to adopt. It will make your staff and business more dynamic and open to new ideas.

The success of any new business initiative is down to a range of factors. It's important that you are constantly measuring, reviewing and finding new opportunities to improve each area of your business development. The use of meaningful metrics is a big shift from what currently happens in business. An environment of carefully selected KPIs gives a framework based on facts, rather than gut feeling. With an understanding of the process, and the numbers, you can clearly identify an area of weakness (or strength), and address as necessary.

Key takeaways

- ✓ Create an inventory of all systems, processes and collateral.

- ✓ Train the relevant staff in each system and create an environment for feedback and improvement

- ✓ Set up systems to measure the KPIs

- ✓ Determine benchmark conversion rates and leading indicators

- ✓ Review performance weekly and monthly

Part 3: Summary

It's clear that there are difficult challenges for the sales industry in terms of its professionalism and perception. An environment of mistrust and suspicion has contributed to a belief that sales is not a noble or valuable profession. This view has permeated into the consciousness of businesses themselves, where management has become one dimensional, focused solely on closing sales, regardless of whether it's right for the buyer or not.

We have come to believe that characteristics such as the 'gift of the gab', being a 'charmer', and the ability to sell anything to anyone, embody what every good salesperson should be. But hopefully this book has demonstrated to you what actually makes smart and efficient sales, and gone someway to dispel the often self-fulfilling and damaging myths.

A salesperson is the conduit between the product or service and the customer. To me that is a position of great privilege. It's often the salesperson's role to find potential customers, qualify their interest and, if appropriate, present their offering. Matching the right clients to the right products is the foundation for a good long-term business. To excel in the role their focus is based on genuinely listening, with interest to the client, and in turn asking insightful questions. Both of which are essential to understanding the real issues, and progressing the sale. It's certainly not about talking the hind legs off a donkey!

Organisations that have recognised the need to develop and improve their sales capabilities have largely done so in a piecemeal fashion. That so few have adopted a team-wide sales system is a worrying symptom of a lack of a coherent strategy. The right way to view your sales function is as one of the most important parts, if not *the* most important, part of your business. This means dedicating time and resources to creating a model based on systems and processes to achieve consistency throughout the company, rather than relying on individuals and the mixed results that produces.

> *"Change before you have to."*
> Jack Welch

The PILOT method has been designed to give a firm foundation for selling effectively. Each of the five steps are fundamental to the success of your business development. Companies that operate a sales framework are able to assess and improve their work in an analytical way. By defining best practice, an organisation can use systems to produce consistency and predictability. The use of metrics makes management much simpler, giving clear targets for improvement and much higher levels of visibility and understanding. Fundamentally, it allows you to see where you and your team are succeeding and failing. An effective sales function starts with the work done in *Positioning*, which lays the groundwork for effective and efficient selling. It's truly perplexing why so many established businesses fail to address these basic business issues and try to sell without them. Whereas new ventures that have implicitly understood those questions, have flourished in recent years.

The challenge for established businesses seems to be greater than ever before as many struggle to adapt to the new selling environment. Some will have time to reposition, but for others the need to address the changes is urgent as competitors and new entrants seek to disrupt the market. New technology has clearly had a big impact on lead generation strategies, but less on face to face negotiating. This is where sales skills are needed, regardless of how you found the lead. Newer tech-savvy businesses still need a process to engage clients and manage their sales teams.

A common misconception has been to focus on selling, specifically closing. While this is an important element it's only part of a bigger picture. It's arguable the focus should be more on lead generation. After all, what use is a salesman with no leads? Actually, what is more fundamental, is seeking to reduce the reliance on individuals. Building a business on a top-rated sales team can be difficult. They are hard to find, expensive and not easy to manage. This model also does little to create value in the business as success is heavily based on a few people.

A more attractive model is one based on systems and processes with staff trained to use them effectively. As well as making a more valuable business, there are other benefits such as consistent and predictable sales results, a reduced reliance on star salespeople, a clear management model and a visible method to assess initiatives.

Technology has profoundly changed the way lead generation is done. The old methods were largely based on pitching to everyone and anyone in the hope that someone would be interested. The new model is about using online methods to target your market scientifically. By creating and sharing valuable content those who are interested can respond and engage. There are many advantages to this model for both buyer and seller. The buyer is more likely to be able to choose the direction they want to follow, having understood the suitability of various providers. The seller can now focus their efforts to on-target clients which means they are much more efficient, and not resorting to 'spray and pray' or 'scattergun' tactics.

"80 percent of success is just showing up."
Woody Allen

While we have acknowledged the over-reliance on sales skills, it's clear they still have a vital part to play in any business. However, the idea that you can only sell if you have some innate ability is a myth. The result is that many potentially good salespeople give up without trying, and those that persist continue to struggle, believing nothing will change. The truth is anyone with the right training and a system to follow can be effective in selling.

The first stage in building a sales system is understanding the steps your clients go through to make a buying decision. When you know this, you can begin to address their concerns and requirements. A sales system is a metaphorical checklist. You tick each stage once completed and progress to the next. Much of this has nothing to do with specific sales skills. It's to do with getting the basics right. This can be as simple as ensuring you are well prepared before a meeting and you 'know your stuff'.

Similarly, follow-ups are done remarkably badly by the sales industry. Even on its own ensuring you have a method to follow-up, will win you more business. Once you have designed a sales system the team has to be trained in it on a continuing basis. To master anything takes practice and sales is no different. Training is a taboo subject for many small businesses. Yet by not making it part of your staff development you are holding back your business.

Whilst this book covers sales to both new and existing clients, the focus for any business is to provide an outstanding product or service to current clients. Without giving your clients value and service you don't have a sustainable business. The best companies have customers who are loyal, long-term supporters who are active in promoting them to their networks. For that to happen there must be a system of delivery that consistently produces delighted clients. This comes down to two essential issues. Does your product effectively solve your client problem and is it delivered in a way the customer is at the very least happy with.

To ensure you can answer these questions, you must learn from your customers what you do well and what you do poorly. Customer feedback is a vastly undervalued and underutilised function as it's often taken as personal criticism. Instead, recognise the key role it plays in business improvement. Use the information gathered to improve and develop your product offerings, and as a benchmark to measure your performance. The Net Promoter Score will give you good visibility, telling you where you are today, and the wider impact and effectiveness of your new and ongoing strategies.

An overriding aim is to shift the emphasis from skills to processes and measurement. Traditionally sales management is littered with ambiguity and limits the ability to manage objectively. *"We had a great meeting with Pete, he's going to do something"* is typical feedback for businesses with no processes. Whereas those following the model in this book are more likely to hear, *"Pete is at stage 4 in the sales process. He's qualified and has now agreed to a demo (in the diary), to decide whether to proceed or not"*. The difference is stark. One is ambiguous and tells you nothing; the other is based on a process and clearly shows the prospect's current position within that process.

With measurement come other benefits. From a management point of view, you can easily see how your team is performing against the system. Are they following it? Are they struggling in a particular area? In addition, sales, like many other business functions, has much built-in inefficiency if not managed and monitored effectively. Such as salespeople wasting time on admin rather than selling.

By using metrics to hold the team accountable you'll see an improvement just by the fact your salespeople are spending more time selling. By breaking down a sale into its component parts, the specific effort required to get a result can be seen. Such as how many leads to get a sale, or how many networking events to secure a meeting? Measurement allows you to understand the effectiveness of your sales activities and the impact of any new initiatives.

"Reinvent your business constantly. The end goal may be the same, but the tools and methods are constantly evolving."

Ken Tucker

Sales, like many professions, is undergoing huge change and much of this can be attributed to technological developments. In a relatively short period of time, we have gone from the 'brick' mobile phone to highly sophisticated and powerful pieces of hardware. At the same time, billion-dollar global mobile phone players have come and gone. The way we work in our personal and business lives is in a constant state of change. Shopping online, working from home and the rise of the 'solepreneur' are all recent, but now common practices.

In the domestic environment the extent to which we engage in new ways of shopping, cooking or exercising is addressed in our own time and down to our personal preferences. But in business a strategy to continue as before, without responding to change, is unrealistic. It's more than apparent that to succeed in today's ultra competitive business environment, you must have the ability and desire, to consistently reposition. This doesn't mean you need to come up with the next dynamic disrupter business model, but it's a dangerous mindset to simply do what you have always done in the hope that it will work out fine in the end.

By working through the five steps in this book, you will have greater certainty about who your target market is and how to engage with them. By putting systems at the heart of your strategy you will transform ambiguity into clarity and build a solid foundation for your business.

183

As you come to the end of the programme you will have covered a lot of new ground. The processes must be set up and the KPIs extracted. While they need not initially be perfect, they should be usable. Your teams need to be fully onside with the processes for the implementation to work, and if you have done this well they will have been engaged from the beginning. New business practices or initiatives are always a struggle to implement when there has been no participation by the staff. Getting their feedback and involving them will make them feel part of the process. Take care not to leave them feeling threatened or overlooked.

Of all the ideas, strategies and content in this book, if nothing else, focus on the following three things:

1. **Develop a deep understanding of your target market:** this enables valuable communication, in a language that is meaningful to your clients.
2. **Use systems and processes:** sales is a science and can give consistent and predictable results but only within a framework of systems and processes.
3. **Be active:** above all, "do something!" as clients won't come and find you. But, to be truly effective, follow all the steps in the programme.

Using this book the additional resources online and lots of determination, fundamental change can be achieved. The result is certainly worthwhile; a well-oiled sales machine producing a consistent supply of leads, converting more prospects and growing existing accounts.

I wish you the very best of luck in developing a long-term thriving and successful enterprise.

Further information

Connect and Feedback

Any questions or comments please drop me an email and I promise to get back to you personally. carlos@thesalesplan.co.uk If you enjoyed the book please give a review on Amazon. Also feel free to connect with me on LinkedIn or Facebook

Online Quiz

Are you on top of your selling? Can you consistently find new leads? Do your clients love what you do? Are your sales teams performing across the board? Take our short online quiz to see how good your sales and business development activities are. Visit - www.thesalesplan.co.uk

Resources

At The Sales Plan website you will find a range of free materials covering each of the five PILOT stages. These include templates, guides, webinars and how-to videos. You can also subscribe to our mailing list to receive ongoing valuable content and offers on our training. Visit - www.thesalesplan.co.uk

PILOT Programme

Want to learn more about PILOT and how we support ambitious midsized companies, great! We'd love to chat with you and find out about your sales challenges. Sign up for a free 15-minute discovery call and we will give you a call at your scheduled time. Book here - www.thesalesplan.co.uk

Boardroom Sessions

We run regular, online and face-to-face boardroom sessions where a small group of business owners come together to discuss and explore their sales activities. These are all about helping other businesses learn new tips, tricks and strategies for improving their sales. To find out more email - info@thesalesplan.co.uk

Acknowledgements and recommended reading

Coaching for Performance, 4th Edition, GROWing Human Potential and Purpose - The Principles and Practice of Coaching and Leadership. By: John Whitmore

Secrets of Closing the Sale. By: ZigZiglar

The Ultimate Question 2.0 How Net Promoter Companies Thrive in a Customer-Driven World By: Fred Reichheld, Rob Markey

The ONE Thing, The Surprisingly Simple Truth Behind Extraordinary Results By: Gary Keller, Jay Papasan

The Five Dysfunctions of a Team A Leadership Fable. By: Patrick Lencioni

The Power of Habit, Why We Do What We Do, and How to Change. By: Charles Duhigg

Key Person of Influence, The Five-Step Method to Become One of the Most Highly Valued and Highly Paid People in Your Industry. By: Daniel Priestley

The 22 Immutable Laws of Marketing. By: Al Ries, Jack Trout

Ego Is the Enemy. By: Ryan Holiday

Getting Naked; A Business Fable About Shedding the Three Fears That Sabotage Client Loyalty. By: Patrick Lencioni

Built to Sell, Creating a Business That Can Thrive Without You. By: John Warrillow

The E-Myth Revisited, Why Most Small Businesses Don't Work and What to Do About It. By: Michael E. Gerber

Oversubscribed. By: Daniel Priestley

Topgrading. By: Bradford D Smart

Uncommon Service. By: Frances Frei& Anne Morriss

Go Naked. By: Michael Smith

Factfulness. By: Hans Rosling, Ola Rosling, AnnaRoslingRönnlund

Influence, The Psychology of Persuasion. By: Robert B. Cialdini

Blue Ocean Strategy, How to Create Uncontested Market Space and Make Competition Irrelevant. By: W. Chan Kim, Renee Mauborgne

Social Media Marketing Workbook: 2018 How to Use Social Media for Business. By: Jason McDonald

Inbound Marketing, Get Found Using Google, Social Media, and Blogs. By: Brian Halligan, Dharmesh Shah

The Inner Game of Tennis, The Classic Guide to the Mental Side of Peak Performance. By: W. Timothy Gallwey

Purple Cow, Transform Your Business by Being Remarkable. By: Seth Godin

The Goal, A Process of Ongoing Improvement - 30th Anniversary Edition. By: Eliyahu M. Goldratt, Jeff Cox

The Sales Acceleration Formula, Using Data, Technology, and Inbound Selling to Go from $0 to $100 Million. By: Mark Roberge

80/20 Sales and Marketing, The Definitive Guide to Working Less and Making More By: Perry Marshall

Scaling Up. How a Few Companies Make It...and Why the Rest Don't, Rockefeller Habits 2.0. By: Verne Harnish

Start with Why How Great Leaders Inspire Everyone to Take Action (Int'l Edit.). By: Simon Sinek

The Seven Habits of Highly Effective People. Powerful Lessons in Personal Change. By: Stephen R. Covey

The Chimp Paradox,The Acclaimed Mind Management Programme to Help You Achieve Success, Confidence and Happiness. By: Prof Steve Peters

Bounce Mozart, Federer, Picasso, Beckham, and the Science of Success. By: Matthew Syed

Just Listen, Discover the Secret to Getting Through to Absolutely Anyone. By: Mark Goulston

"Carlos expertly disaggregates what can be seen as a complex selling process into an easily understandable and intuitive system built on five key elements. His PILOT methodology will improve performance in any organization that adopts it. If you want to develop a deeper understanding of your target market, develop a more predictable business development funnel and improve the consistency of your results then this book will show you how."

Michal Smith. Author and Vice President, Global Marketing Align Technology

"The core of any activities is to provide value to your community or clients. When you manage a growing and influencing entity, you need to be able to assess how your team, and your sales department in particular, are performing. This is a comprehensive but completely practical book, enabling business owners and managers the ability to create highly effective sales systems."

Jean-Philippe Perraud. General Director of NEDonBoard, The Professional Body for NEDs & Board Members, listed on GOV.uk

"For many companies, sales is a never-ending cycle of frustration, wasted time and money. In The Sales Plan, Carlos has produced a simple but effective approach to creating a sales environment that delivers results and is scalable. Essential reading for any midsized business owner!"

Alexander Seery. Author and founder, Shifts to Success

"This book proves that any organisation can sell, provided they build a sales infrastructure. This means starting from the 'bottom up'. Who are your clients? What are their challenges? And how do you engage them? This book covers these fundamental stages in a clear, methodical and practical way, transforming businesses into selling experts."

Stephen Connolly. Writer and MD Plain Money

"In an ever more competitive world being able to effectively sell products and services in a way that is truly relevant to your target markets has never been more important. The Sales Plan provides a clear concise and proven path to achieving that for all types of organisations including, retailers, manufacturers and providers of professional services."

Andrew Glen. MD Riverside Greetings

Printed in Great Britain
by Amazon

35652309R00119